M000234616

Michel Serres

Variations
on the Body

Variations sur le corps by Michel Serres
© Le Pommier 1999

Translated by Randolph Burks
as *Variations on the Body*

First Edition
Minneapolis © 2011, Univocal Publishing
Published by Univocal
123 North 3rd Street, #202
Minneapolis, MN 55401
www.univocalpublishing.com

Designed & Printed by Jason Wagner

Distributed by the University of Minnesota Press

ISBN 9781937561062
Library of Congress Control Number 2011944716

Contents

Metamorphosis

I'm walking over ground of a gradually steepening pitch. At a certain point, I pause and start using my hands; the real mountain begins. I'm climbing. Do I, as soon as my back slopes forward, return to the state of the quadruped? Almost: my body transforms; feet become hands and my two manual grips secure balance. *Homo erectus*, the standing man, of recent date, reverts back to the one from whom he is descended: the archaic quadrumane. This thunderbolt recollection became so black, in me, that I no longer fear to speak of the beast; I remember who we were.

Everyone knows the risks incurred in the mountains: even when careful and cautious, alpinists die there from accidents. Where then does that intense sense of security come from that's experienced by those who, calm, devote themselves to a passion reputed to be dangerous? Anxiety, of course, occurs before the climb, just as fear returns after; but during it, the body progresses, on the rock face, as though it were protected. But, leaving aside guides, pitons, ropes and partners, by what, by whom?

HUMANITY AND ANIMALS

Stretch out your arms and legs: your twenty fingers and toes attain in space a large rectangular frame or a circle – your starfish, octopus or gibbon's maximal hold on the world. Your active force and sensibility radiate at the extreme points of this figure. Let these rivets hold, and you no longer have any need for bed or hearth; you inhabit this square: place, dwelling, niche. Move your limbs, now, and feel form around you, starting from this flat frame, an invisible and mobile parallelepiped – cube, prism or large paving stone – equipped with its sides, edges and vertices, a ball even or perhaps a sphere, whose elements – the points, lines and planes, which I would prefer to call already geometric, since they ensure mastery of the earth – go into the construction of the animal's natal house, its first refuge, the originary architecture of its primitive building. Curled up within the womb formed by the curves of force traced out by its four hands, the ape has no need for a roof. The body's back and upper parts protect it. The animal inhabits this tunic, skin, membrane or envelope that is its relation to a world which is to correspond to it. I've frequented these too often not to be aware of them. Who climbs the rock face? Not a visible body exposed to the void, but, precisely, this mobile extensible ball inside of which the simian organism reposes. Before launching out, I assess the wall and see the invisible web of holds that line up with my possible grasp; the ball sticks, adapted, on the route thus woven. I believe I understand the spider, whose net projects afar – element by element – the aforementioned tunic induced by its eight arthropod legs, since, often, I've been transformed into a daddy long-legs on a rock, or hanging, on rappel, at the end of a rope. How could we have forgotten this elementary and animal relation to the world?

THE BODY IN ITS NASCENT STATE

During his regression to this pre-human state, the climber is, therefore, sheltered in an archaic, invisible, elastic, obliging uterus, whose variable paving stone contains and protects his entire body which is, then, slumbering inside the prehensions and supports that stay awake for it – just like his head, that stupid animal, which is, then, sleeping: I know how things are with not thinking. The animal stretches out in the prenatal. When the slope levels out, the alpinist gets up again. Then, just as the chick breaks the shell's vault with its beak or the drowsy joey delivers itself from the parental pouch and wakes on its hind legs, likewise, to give birth to man – erect biped or little girl on the march – our quadrumane ancestor had to break open that membrane, a shirt slipping along the trunk, falling, to the ground, in a crumpled pile, a shirt thus reduced, then, to the support polygon, that small clumsy handkerchief, sometimes punctual and null, starting from which two hands, two feet, plus a head began in disequilibrium, out of plumb perpendicularity, movement and freedom – the two hands strangely useless, the two feet stumbling over pebbles, the head in the air, naked, given birth to, come forth, given over to the wind, the sun, the cold, in pure nature, therefore in danger. Suddenly, it had to start thinking... but of what? Of constructing a house with its new hands. The very first cogito was a plan for a refuge to recover the lost ball. This is why we seek a roof; this is why we inhabit. The human, standing, has just been born.

The Body in Motion

Penetrated by the snow, overcome by the sun, bent against the wind, reduced to silence by shortness of breath, the roped party is therefore ascending the wall. The least false step and gravity, swiftly, takes its revenge. The body relies only on its valor and the generosity of those who expect the same in return. This fair harshness teaches the truth of things, of others and oneself, without pretense. Exacting corporal exercises kick off the program of first philosophy wonderfully with an immediate decision, one cutting short all doubt: high on the mountain, hesitation, going in the wrong direction, lies and cheating are equivalent to death.

Written or spoken, repeated without danger, language, conversely, causes the proliferation of parrots who, immobile, fidget and reproduce. The other is reduced to nothing in it, by dead messages, and the thing is reduced to its recording media – wax, screen, paper – lastly oneself is reduced to its neurons, to the I, to thought. The risk of truth disappears, whereas the world, inimitable, exacts movements and actions whose pertinence it immediately sanctions, and the group destroys itself there in proportion to its lies. But, in fair exchange, this world shows its phenomena, in all obviousness, and gives its data for free. Faced with the naked rock, the naked body cheats as little as does an automatic machine equipped with its software: a faithful, in these two cases, simulation, a lying one everywhere else.

I've never known how to express the ego, nor describe consciousness. The more I think, the less I am; the more I am I, the less I think and the less I act. I don't seek myself as subject, stupid project; only things and others are found. Among these, a little less thing and much less other, is my body. In order to speak fairly of it, I began long ago with *The Five Senses*: the skin, hearing's pinna, the two non-verbose tongues of flavors and kissing, the visit on the move of the world's landscapes... sensuality's delectable pleasures. Clever, hypocritical and lying, the speech that explores who I am – full of vanity when it fidgets within the hidden recesses of a warm and lazy interior – again becomes instructive and fair (I insist upon once again taking up this adjective) as soon as the body exposes itself to cold, danger and death, in the most intense of osseous, muscular, perceptual, metabolic, respiratory, sanguineous, total activities: neither the body nor speech, then, can dream, strut, cheat or lie. Let's go.

THE BODY ASSOCIATES THE SENSES

The ascent begins before the dawn; climbing reveals space. Flying in an airplane, the traveler's eyes widen, sometimes, to the size of the windows, while – slumped in its narrow seat in the rapid passenger cabin – his body sleeps. This is indeed a flyover vision: however large the landscape, below, may present itself, it forms a spectacle, like at the cinema, where the viewers remain passive and seated in a dark room, reduced to the gaze, the only activity in a flesh as absent as a black box. The animated eye

8

overhanging a quasi-dead organism produces almost incorporeal sensations, already abstract. When, on the contrary, hands are squeezing blood out of the rock, when chest and stomach, legs and genitals, stay parallel to the wall, when back, muscles, nervous, digestive and sympathetic systems are engaging themselves, together and without reservation, in the material approach of the relief, in a relation of apparent struggle and real seduction, so that the stone, to the touch, loses its hardness so as to gain, loved, an astonishing softness, vision – even broad – loses its flyover distance and concerns the entire body, as though the totality of the organism, become lucid, contributed to the gaze, while the eyes go a little black; so what, from above, remains spectacle, becomes integrated into the body whose size grows, in return, to the gigantic dimensions of the world. The ensemble of holds contributes to apprehension: global grasp and vague fear. Sight reposes on touch. Tissues and bones become so elastic I think I'm touching the valley, three thousand meters below, with my fingers, and, already, the peak, before having reached it. While my skin, extensible, is fitting itself closely over the region to the point of covering it, the contemplative or theoretical soul, dormant, is shrinking and taking refuge in the forgetfulness of abstraction. This second vision entirely reverses the flyover kind: the living eye in the dead body produces theory, in a sort of self-evidence; does he see it inside out, the mountaineer whose gaze is growing black in a white body which, living, contemplates, by clasps and caresses, the entire universe it covers right side out?

The body in motion federates the senses and unifies them within itself. For this corporal vision, this touch that, by a wondrous transubstantiation, changes the rock face into flesh, unceasingly enchanted, in the absence of language, by tacit music. To carry off a mountain climb without tiring, even an exacting one, it's enough, in the silence, never to lose some theme and its variations: they send precious assurances of balance from the external ear to its internal neighbor. Sustained, this unheard of song rises from the body, in the grip of rhythmic movement – heart, breath and regularity – and seems to emerge from the receptors of the muscles and joints, in sum, from the sense of the gestures and movement, invading the body first, then the environment, with a harmony which celebrates its grandeur, adapting to it the very body which emits it, then abounds in it, filled. Taciturn since the beginning of the world, the earth and sky, the cold shadow and the mauve predawn light strewing with pink the ice corridors and needles of rock, together sing the glory. Daylight spreads through the enormous volume. I hear the divine invading the Universe.

The Written Body

I have for a long while thought that I had inherited
the trade of my fathers, on account of the slowness of
the plowed furrows aligned on the page, with great
efforts from the arm, wrist, arching back and the time
begun before the dawn: a writer, I lived like the archaic
peasant of the boustrophedon, an old word meaning
that the oxen pulling the plow turn around at the
end of the furrow in order to begin the following
one, parallel to it but opposite in direction. Now if
plowing relentlessly carries on a labor whose linearity
only demands patience, what do we do about the
unexpected obstacles, such as the demonstration that
hits a stumbling block, the missing documentation
or the development suddenly frozen by some sterile
drying up, or worse, by the ugliness which, with
its clumsiness, ruins the sentence? We need, here,
technical prowess, doubly assured belays, there,
we need grace, lastly, more flexibility and strength,
depending on the degree of difficulty or the thinness
of the holds: here I am on the rock wall, will I pass the
difficult section or won't I? The discontinuous course
becomes surprising, beneath an unexpected sky. Thus
writing resembles mountain climbing more than level
plowing. The page tilts upward, inspired, less flat than
the field, soon vertical and exciting. Lying on the table,
the page in the past resembled a flat, open area; but,
now, the computer's smooth screen forms a rock face:

what holds are there to grab onto? Then yes, the entire body gathers itself, from the feet to the cranium: head and belly, muscles and genitalia, back and thighs, sweat and presence of mind, emotion, attention and valor, persevering slowness, the five senses assembled by that of movement, but suddenly, lightning speed, inspiration and concentration, demand for silence... the true subject of writing clings to the page-wall, climbs the screen, engages with them as a hand-to-hand wrestler – fair, respectful, familiar, enchanted, amorous... – but in such a way that if by chance he let go of a hold or didn't see it, he would fly, a disarticulated jumping jack, to the bottom of beauty. An entrancing page chants the body; a bad one reeks of an arid head.

Because writing is no more forgiving than the mountain, most walkers-writers have themselves preceded by guides and surrounded by ropes: citations-belays, notes-mountain huts, references-pitons. The sham craft consists in the multiplication of proper names; the genuine writer's craft demands a solitary engagement from the entire body and its sole singularity. Gymnastic exercise, a rather austere diet, life in the open air, a thousand practices of strength and flexibility, on the whole, alpine climbs, for writing, are as good as ten libraries. Specific, distinctive, original, the whole body invents; the head likes to repeat. Head, stupid; body, brilliant.

Why didn't I learn its creative force sooner? Why didn't I understand when I was younger that only the glorious body could be taken for real? This is why, in the twilight of my life, I am singing it, for the edification of my successors. What are you going to do in the high mountains, at your age? Prepare my writing. Study, learn, certainly – something of it will always stay with you – but, above all, train the body and have confidence in it, for it remembers everything without weight or overloading. Our divine flesh alone distinguishes us from machines; human intelligence can be distinguished from artificial intelligence by the body, alone.

PANIC

Thirty-five years ago, I had to give knock-out shots to several sailors, as well as, alas, the ship's doctor, who were spreading panic aboard the vessel in distress, on which we almost went down with all hands in the eastern Mediterranean, in a tempest; one wave, high as a mountain, was all that could be seen. They were choked by the throes of a mortal terror, and their madness was being transmitted to those around them with lightning speed. The quasi-divine seizure of an organism by panic is similar to demonic possession; master of relations, some demon takes hold of all those who appear on the stage of its theater, in a dance uncoordinated to the point of paralysis, amid the cries, rictus, vomiting, icy and copious sweats, the tetanization and then collapse of the muscles, the relaxations of the sphincter, the stench of the appalling trails, the death pangs. This intense fear, the true fear, unleashed by a monster that alienates your body proper, differs greatly from the playacting of representation: the night before the climb, allow yourself the luxury of anxiety and, in fact, tremble, don't sleep, abandon yourself in anticipation to disarray, all of which is of no consequence, since you never leave bed: pretend apprehensions, more or less pleasant. But once, standing, you don your headlamp, you have no right to fear. Because the true fear will be at stake; not the night fear, nor the theatrical fear written about in books, but the fear produced by the guest who strikes down, fells, kills, and threatens to haunt, hence to murder your ropemates. Here, moral law rejoins the religious, the social rule of politeness and several precepts of bodily cleanliness: you cannot inflict on the climbing team a soft, whining sack of excrements whose passivity, inertia and weight expose the others to the danger of death, or worse, nausea. Don't confuse the two fears: the one that has no object, a perverse variety of a passive pleasure, with the true fear, a sacrificial prelude to collective murder and suicide.

Joy

Everyone, someday, experiences the unbearable pain, accompanied by anguish, of losing a part of his integrity: an arm, a woman loved, one's country. Are there more exquisite tortures than those that rack a phantom limb? The slightest subtraction extracts radical suffering from our undivided sum. Existence scatters our flesh across space. My body no longer lives except as the remainder of separations. One must have plunged into these abysses of pain in order to begin to understand, as though by a more than overcompensated symmetry, coitus. If, in the cavity of this removal, minus one tortures the whole, plus one exceeds surplus, as though beyond a summital maximum. The peak of the high mountain fills the cavity of the abyss with its overflow and overfills the slope, vertical and vertiginous, down which pain doesn't stop falling. Yes, losing one's grip and falling initiates a long flesh-exposed slide over the impersonal edge of an abyss, a trip that replaces the brief descent of a short step toward the grave in the familiar cemetery. Whereas, fractured, a totality ceaselessly skids away from its former tranquil, full, happy quietude, now, conversely, a superaliment, a supercapacity surpasses it, and a superadded superelevation substitutes for a superdeepening. Surprise, a humbly superhuman or physically supernatural joy – broad, broad, broad –

unexpectedly arrives, and, superb, super-soars and superabounds. Life superlives.

During a few ascents of the Écrins Massif or that of Mont Blanc, by night; after the descent of the Matterhorn, and this over two days; or on other occasions still, rare ones, I was suddenly inundated, filled, saturated, satiated, flooded over, thunderstruck with such a lofty elation, continuous and sovereign, that I thought my chest was bursting, that my entire body was levitating, present in all the space of the world entirely present in me. Pleroma of exultation. There was nothing artificial in that experience, since it occurred at times when I was eating little and drinking only water, and since all my attention, nervous and muscular, was required so as not to fall: thus the ecstasy arose during an active period when reality, hard, was mobilizing the entire body. I suspect the pathological analyses of mysticism of a malicious ignorance, because they overturn its strength into sickly weakness and its action into passivity. Costly drugs or mental illnesses, to be sure, produce hallucinations whose cardboard scenery caricatures the authentic ecstasies of the healthy. Saint Theresa of Avila, Saint Francis of Assisi, with athletic bodies, walked hundreds of kilometers in all kinds of weather, across the hard topographies of Spain and Italy, all the while strewing them with foundations of masonry, hardworking, not sick, but more than normal, powerful, experts in the techniques of the body. Saintliness follows health, just as knowledge does action. Ecstasy presupposes equilibrium and, far from destroying it, surpasses it, imparting the real as such, live and direct, refusing substitutes. Jubilant exultation does not emerge from melancholy, but from immediate contact with the rock. In general, creation does not arise from torpor, nor from narcosis, but from training, and it is rewarded with supergrowth. Contrary to our legends, the work emerges from an excess of superpower. The joy felt increases with the effort consented; this goes all the way to the limits.

The in shape athlete, the trained gymnast, the active worker, the mountaineer at the apex of his exactingness, in the attentive precision of his relation to the ice, during the total engagement of their bodies – sweat, tension, breath, flexibility, adaptation – suddenly transform, rare, unexpectedly, into seraphim and benefit from the emotions felt by the angels who, themselves – transfigurations of champions – enjoy more-than-perfect bodies rather than flabby languor on some divan with clouds for cushions. Exercise the body as preparation for the ascent to heaven. Strong and sturdy legs are needed for the ascent of the wall on which the mystical festival of the Ascension is experienced.

The climb, therefore, begins at the summit. A special torture, careful down-climbing requires that retention be played off against gravity and that one boldly rush toward the attractor void, but through mastering its law, reversing therefore the work of the muscles, putting the back in place of the front, the knees in their popliteal crease, sending the eyes beneath the toes, making the entire body go cross-eyed in chiasma – the front, the back; the top, the bottom; the left, the right – opening out or unrolling lastly, unfolding strength instead of drawing it toward oneself, in extension rather than traction. Is the mountain intersected by a gigantic mirror, so that upon crossing the summit the climb pushes us into the space of its own image, making reversed jumping jacks of us? No training prepares for this monstrous turnabout.

Thus, we didn't know and so learn on the descent ridge unfurling in front of us like a banner luffing in the wind that, sunk even deeper than the quadrumane into the depths of evolution, we're still univalve mollusks: periwinkle, limpet or barnacle attached to the rock, whelk, cowrie.... Fragile, precious and soft, our eyes, indeed, our mouth, solar plexus, breasts, belly and genitals, comfortable within the softness of the anterior side, live and protect themselves along a tough back, vaulted like a carapace, whose bony heels, projecting shoulder-blades, spinal column – curved and framework-straight – together go into the construction, along with its compact buttocks and the neck's rigorous nape, of a dense and incurvate wall, in and against which our weaknesses let themselves go. Soft being in a hard there, though mobile.

The body lies down and sleeps in this shell in which it leans back; the anterior organs inhabit like a house the posterior valve, a shell that's solid like the inert and dark to perception, a quasi natural niche that moves, pivots or leans a little, depending on the person, to the right or to the left, so that we repose in the favorite side of the back whose strength, like a foundation, supports, from shoulder to trousers, the conquests and enterprises of the front, so feeble, puny, delicate and tender that without this invincible backing, it would never permit itself such audacities. When the courageous person faces and the coward flees, the first exposes the soft, the second offers only the hard. During the attempt on the wall, rock and back then form two solid shells – one belonging to us, the other the world – inside of which the soft, hypocritical and intelligent inhabitant of the shadows always takes shelter; does the periwinkle turn into a clam, cockle, oyster, scallop or maxima clam? I know the wound where, inside, the pearl grows.

Better: by sending its shelters back to the rear, the body, standing, remembers the roof that used to protect the upper parts of the quadrumanous animal it once was: a kind of tortoise whose carapace has interiorized as a skeleton. Observe to what extent this quadruped resembles a house, and how, conversely, the house mimics this very same four-footed beast, both surrounded by bone, tile and brick, above, all around and on the sides. The soft, underneath: belly and kitchen, heart, genitals and heating... inhabits the hard: back and roof, thorax and frame, columns and legs. By standing up, the fragile is exposed. Does our evolution and, perhaps, that of the whole of life consist of this fearful, timid and reckless boldness: going outside toward the world of things, not remaining at rest, at home; moving out? Being born: exposing the fragile to the harsh, the warm to the icy, the soft to the hard and the tender to violence; this is what it means to know.

Thus I sometimes dream that, unlike our brother animals, delivered over – fangs, claws and beaks – to Darwinian laws, mankind has protected the weak instead of killing them, since, standing, it was itself exposing its weaknesses, especially its pregnant female. This latter leads me to think that, in the quadrupedal position, her genitalia are displayed from behind, while that of the male are concealed below his belly; when both stand up, everything is reversed, the male displays what the female hides. Our sexuality is different from that of animals and our ancestors, separated from us by that reversal which began with our upright posture. Going from the position *a tergo* to an unexpected face to face brings about smiling looks, a delightful amiability, new words; the pushing and shoving ends up in the court of love.

The postural reversal is also pertinent for gait and bearing; as a runner or nimble walker, I inhabit the muscles of my thighs and the tendons of my ankles – the vibrating cables and strong columns of my port as well as my transport – just as much as I used to reside, a powerful athlete, in the shell and roof of my dorsal parts. Yes, softer, the top rests on the bottom, harder, the way the front leans on the back. But, by traversing the mirror at the points on the summit where universal attraction for it becomes overturned, this univalve mollusk, this demilune stretched out in its dorsal hammock, would have to become shell on its soft side, consciousness or waking on its hard or obscure face, powerful tanned leather where it is flaccid, or, better still, the inhabitant would have to become the nest, and the walls of the house the tenant itself. No known learning, no known training conducts us to such a feat, hence the torture of the descent, feared even by the best trained. Finding itself condemned to remain for so long an unconscious shell or roof, often aching, the back complains and dreams in its turn, of integrating another valve, having become a subject again. On balance, in how many emergency blankets, tunics, supports or foundations, frameworks, mountain huts, houses interior or exterior to our bodies, will we search for a habitat; in how many niches will we live, sleep, will we walk and work before conceiving the courage to give ourselves over to the world?

Ethics, in Passing

The descent gives us a body seized by letting go, whereas the climb up gives free rein to the common centripetal passions, such as: clinging to handholds, acquiring, drawing by means of nerves and muscles an object toward oneself and oneself toward an objective, arriving or desiring. Seizing, devouring, consuming. Down-climbing leaves behind. Gesture, then, becomes generous. Starting from clenched hands, the arms open out, you'd think that they give and no longer take, that they abandon the mountain to the given, to that perpetual given men have been capturing, since the history of their schemes began its performance, without tearing the least little bit of wear out of it. An hour of frost erodes the wall more than a thousand caresses by feverish and groping hands. Trust those who let go – the wisest among us – trust those who descend, who leave behind, who can but don't, trust the detached, trust those who give way, trust the poor and those who live apart.

Those who ascend, on the contrary, and who stretch out toward the desired seizure neither do, nor think about anything other than what favors their appetite. Culture, civilization, wisdom, beauty, even thought begins with letting go, with the arm gesture that relaxes, centrifugal. Active, enthusiastic, courageous, dynamic, willful – begin nevertheless by desiring strongly. Otherwise, might as well praise passivity, another form of the animal state. Ascending, first, seizing, wanting, sweating, happily taking your fill by the armful; once past the summit, removing, taking off, parting with, divesting yourself, this is the proper course of time. The profile of life given in those old prints, red and blue, formerly hung in country kitchens, in which young and good-looking figures were merrily ascending up to the mid-point of existence, so as to descend afterwards, ugly and aged, the other side of a triangle formed – its vertex upward – by the cradle, adult triumph and the grave, this traverse traces out that profile within the space of a day; but at the same time it teaches that morality and wisdom also follow this evolutionary history, since, fresh and joyful, vernal, belonging to the morning, certain active virtues accompany birth, starts and beginnings, since sunny like high noon, other virtues, strong and serene, shine at the apex, and since lastly, gilded like the sunset, contemplative, the final virtues

gently gather their thoughts so as to attain silence. I
will die from a descent.

How the Body Stands and Walks

I have my guide to thank and him alone – what then
did you do, Mother? – for being able to stand and
knowing how to walk. When this learning takes place
at around the age of forty, the body is surprised by the
delay, but is instructed by it just as much. On the rare
occasions when they emerge from their automobile
shells, our contemporaries walk over leveled ground,
so that their head remains in the clouds, I mean
to say outside their legs, while these latter pedal
along automatically. Technology has removed so
many obstacles to their strolling for so long, even
tenuous ones, that Marcel Proust was given raptures
of memory the moment the paving stones became
uneven, forgetting that the highway department had
recently smoothed them. Once, some Carioca friends
asked me, in all seriousness, whether there were
special schools in Europe where we learned to forget
the natural soft gait, so as to set ourselves walking,
artificial and hard; the mountain compels me to recall
their intelligent distinction, corporal or computing,
between hard and soft: doubtless they meant that
they walked, themselves, with eyes placed along
their tendons and muscles, assuring a spiritual gaze
between two flexibilities, while the aforementioned

Occidentals, stiff and articulated, perch on the bony stilts of the tibia, on the crutches of the fibula, talus and calcaneus, completely stilted. These Rio dancers, did they know, at that time, before I did, that our joints and muscles are furnished with refined sensors? That the sense that most confederates the other senses remains the sense of balance and movement? The step sets up, in effect, a cycle that, if maintained in proper condition, links sight to the sole of the foot's sense of touch, then quickly sends the latter back to the former, which, after monitoring and anticipation, returns it with more pace; the eye caresses the rock before the gait touches it and confirms, in response, the unencumberedness of the gaze – so that the pupil almost touches and the arch of the foot practically sees. Curved and flexible, knees bent, this circle and it alone perambulates, connecting the toes to the eyes and back again, and not that stiff stick whose waist eternally separates a blind heel from a hypocritical nape of the neck. Far from being an immutable segment of straight line combing and raking space, as hedge posts would, the gait inhabits the elastic and mobile continuously resumed ellipse of a water magnifying glass. Second reversal: sight touches and touch sees. Break the cycle even for a moment, you fall. Sight walks or life ceases. He who doesn't know how to walk puts one foot in front of the other; he who does puts an eye in front of each shoe.

Now this fluid bubble, readily, centers itself as though along a water level, whereas a stake tumbles over as soon as the ground slopes a little. Starting at what angle, when climbing, do you begin using your hands and, when descending, stand again? This question immediately determines your age and hominin condition. The diversity, here, is laughable: one person remains on all fours on a slope his body still considers to be vertical, while his neighbor, finding himself well and truly on the horizontal, has been on his feet for some time. Thus a quadrumane chimpanzee and a *sapiens sapiens* are found in the neighborhood of one another, within the same species. You recognize the alpinist, that man who knows how to walk, by his risen body. Standing erect is therefore acquired and has more to do with the ear – no doubt, but also the entire body and pleasure – than the eye. At the same time as learning to walk over steep, difficult, capricious grounds, you must learn to find your seat there; then and then only, when all the the skin of the foot sends the entire body a hundred delectable messages of velvet, wool and silken comfort, do you learn how one becomes hominin, banishing from yourself the univalve, the quadruped and the ape – an erect animal, a risen child, an adult person expelling everything that remains infantile. Leaving childhood and the animal, what joy at last: the body gets its kicks.

Sketched out towards the end of *The Five Senses*, the classification of the basic forms of sensual pleasure – breathing, waking, jumping, walking, running, carrying... – was deficient, since it didn't take into account standing balance. Not stable, but unstable, better still, metastable, invariant through variations, this equilibrium is constructed like a refuge or a habitat, composed like a musical score, over fragile epicycles or minuscule rapid ellipses, planed cams, minor stumblings recovered from, differentials of angles or of deviations quickly returned to the peace of the smooth and even, a sloped roof but, in all, flat... arrhythmia and prosody, odd and even, anharmonic seventh chords resolved, mixed consonance and dissonance, disquieted calls followed by thundering responses... these are the wonderful cycles of reciprocal support between the labyrinth of the inner ear, charged with bearing, and the spiral volutes of the external ear, which hears and produces music, converging in a black and secret center, common to both these networks, where I suddenly discover the solution to the dark mysteries of the union of the soul that hears language and the bearing body... disquieted experience, certainly, since the second word of this phrase designates, as does *existence*, a deviation from equilibrium, yes, destabilization followed by ecstasy, and since the first word expresses yet another deviation from quietude, yes, infinitesimals of exaltations – oh, our primordial elations, our delicate delectations! After the musical offertory hymn, might the Word itself have arisen from the uprightness, disquiet and quiet, of the flesh?

RETURNING FULFILLED

Upon my return, I doze, lying, in the garden. Unfolded, unrolled, laid out flat so they're no longer pocketed, the tissues of my lungs, they say, would cover a large region. But as they are – folded, multiplied – my bronchioles would instead nicely mold a seacoast of jagged rocks or some arête crowned with irregular spires. This allows me to breathe freely in the wide open space, whether I sleep, as I will tomorrow, by the shores of the ocean and wind, or wake, as I did yesterday, on the capricious turrets of the Matterhorn's pyramid, the thorax of the Earth. The nerve endings that complete the brain's hold over the organism, I know them to be so entangled that if, the cranial bones being open, I should gently remove the soft, gray and white mass of the brain from its abode, my entire body, knotted, attached, drawn, petit points by petit points, by thick shocks of hair, inextricable and complete, would turn inside out, like the fingers of a glove, to display, on the reverse side of the epidermis, that dense, innumerable, complex, admirable network that I intensely feel allows me to think out to the minuscule extremities of the sensible.

The endings of the blood vessels that complete the heart's hold over the organism, I know them to be so entangled that if, the thorax bones being open, I should gently remove the red and soft cardiac mass from the mediastinum, my entire body, knotted, attached, drawn, petit points by petit points, by thick shocks of hair, inextricable and complete, would turn inside out, like the fingers of a glove, to display on the reverse side of the epidermis, that dense, innumerable, complex, admirable network that I intensely feel, that I know warms me up and nourishes me out to the minuscule extremities of life. Does the place of this latter fold endlessly over itself? Around this body and its multiple nets, swaying in the chaos of the turbulent avenues of air, fluttering in the squalls of the wind, the branches and branchings, boughs and twigs, leaves and stomata displayed by strata, of three poplars, glistening with wet sparkles, dart upright into the volume of the blue sky. Our places of life, small, cast and mix their admirable networks, so complex and fringed down to the subliminal that they pose algorithmically intractable problems, mix them, as I was saying, with the admirable networks, inert or living, which, here and there, are distributed throughout the Universe – flamboyant mountain, fractal littoral, flows of winds and waters, groupings of turbulence, trees with their foliage.

Here is the beginning of a description, reasonable and felt, of sensation, by places and folds, proximities, penetrations and mixtures. But if no one knows how to handle the problems posed by just one of these lattices, how can we imagine resolving those their mixtures have in store for us? That intelligence may be artificially reconstructed, certainly, I don't see anything particularly astonishing in that, but flesh, the sensible, the body? Incarnation is the pinnacle of the concrete as well as of the most abstract knowledge. Our bodies thus have at their disposal a sufficient advance, a margin of peace before the learned seriously disturb us from our climbs and our sensorial siestas, before they trouble our cultural joys of sapience and sagacity, welcomed once again, without logic or calculation, by strong wind and broad sunshine on this first afternoon of August during which, just descended from the summit of the Matterhorn, stretched out in my garden, on the ground, I exquisitely mix my inmost extremities, minuscule, with the multiple external tremblings of the treetops, thirty meters above the ground. If spaces, therefore, if habitable places multiply, inside and out, and are knotted together like the various times – my time, the Earth's, history's and evolution's – how many more days and nights will my flesh of language, tints and music remain on the apex or arêtes of the hypnotic mountain, dancing in unstable equilibrium on their knifeblade edge, an immense vibrating reed in the lips of the wind?

Potential

No seated professor taught me productive work, the only kind of any worth, whereas my gymnastics teachers, coaches and, later, my guides inscribed its very conditions into my muscles and bones. They teach what the body can do. Do you want to write, do research, live a work-producing life? Follow their advice and example, namely: that nothing can withstand training, the ascesis of which repeats rather unnatural gestures (the drop kick, the tennis serve, the Fosbury flop, yoga...) and makes effortless the necessary virtues of concentration (basketball, the high jump), courage (rugby), patience, the mastery of anxiety, in the mountains for instance; that no work can be produced without observing the same rule, quasi-monastic, by time schedule as the high level athlete: a life subjected to the body's rhythms, a strict sleep hygiene, a drug-free diet; that the researcher who cheats or lies neither finds nor invents, just as the high jumper neither cheats nor lies with gravity... this iron law turns its back on every practice on the part of the collectives whether professional, political, media, academic... that crowns mobsters and puts the mediocre in power. Respect the thing itself that, alone, commands and not opinion, this above all else teaches the work-producing life. Whatever the activity you're involved in, the body remains the medium of intuition, memory, knowing, working and above all invention. A mechanical procedure can replace any of the understanding's operations, never the actions of the body. In a nonetheless intellectual trade, no one has helped me the way my gymnastics instructors have... to them, all of my grateful respect.

My Teachers

That's what my personal life owes them; this is what we owe them, in our collective existence. Team spirit is built by controlling our competitive fire and respecting the referee's decisions; team sports teach us to fight, together and juridically, with our opponents, against aggressiveness, ours and theirs; how many young men would wind up in prison without rugby, without boxing, wrestling, gymnastic apparatus, judo? The rampages of the soccer hooligans reveal the origin of the sporting event, the same as for tragedy: since the dawn of history, we have gathered so as to fight together against violence, by contemplating it; but it continuously reappears, especially in the very places where our best remedies are played, remedies which thus remain temporary and prone to wearing out: we have to begin again. He who has the ball thus learns the role of the victim and to escape it passes the ball off to others, but this must be done under the right conditions, so as not to bring the punishment down upon his comrade.

Alas, drugs and money, thus new ways of cheating, destroy such precious teachings; hence the most archaic practices: the sale of men and women, the return of slavery, the degradation by overtraining and the demand for victory... human sacrifices destined for the exaltation of nations and finance. The morality I exhibit initially tumbles toward a lumpenproletariat economy and an ethnology of the sacrificial spectacle. Yes, the noble sport, that of guides, which makes bodies blossom and teaches the physical and moral virtues, is opposed to the ignoble sport, that of money, which cultivates the contrary virtues and spreads fascism. Competition is excellent, when it improves people but atrocious when obeying a certain social Darwinism whose ideal of the strongest, purely animal, reverses the process of hominization, which from its origin progresses, on the contrary, by protecting the weak.

For the most part, sports clubs, in fact, never win a single championship; by far most athletes never wear a medal around their neck... in their vast majority, athletes lose: this is what their ascesis teaches; losing, to be sure, against the others, but winning in the things themselves and for oneself.... By teaching us to despise Nazi victory hymns, coaches then become the best educators in politics and human evolution: to them, our grateful respect.

What can our bodies do? Almost anything.

Weakness

How many of the learned, on the contrary, announce that the hominin body, feeble and placed by nature in the weakest position among all the living, cannot do very much. This asinine idea dates back at least three thousand years without the most constant experience preventing it from braying; let some foolishness escape from a respected philosopher and twenty-five centuries of education will repeat it, thickening it even with armored commentaries. That on the contrary, in fact, with the hand, the foot, the heart, nerves and muscles... in dexterity, strength, flexibility, adaptation and wind... sailors, mothers, mountaineers, acrobats, surgeons, athletes, wrestlers, travelers, magicians, virtuosos... outmatch, in performances of all kinds and in every strictly physical discipline, the entire animal kingdom whose species specialize in definite gestures... that the diverse ethnic groups are scattered across the planet, confronting the most extreme climates which only evolution, over millions of years, enables the beasts to endure... that each genus only executes a rigid and limited program, while, freer, humans are constantly planning unexpected feats... this general experience doesn't seem to have struck these philosophies – busy repeating the litany of our weaknesses – with wonder. Whose body are they talking about?

So know its incredible capabilities: tireless and made for scarcity, the human animal can put its back into the oars for months to cross the Pacific, work its entire life under the disapproval of its peers, spend seven stormy winter days on a vertical wall of ice in the high mountains or thirty years of illness to compose, in suffocation and suffering, a work of music, traverse Greenland or Antarctica in frigid temperatures deadly to any other animal, fight against a criminally perverse government to the point of toppling – the human animal all by itself – the entire collective contract that conditions it; some old men run a hundred kilometers in a few hours, while an adult male lion quits after sixty meters, from overheating or to catch his breath; those in dire poverty survive in such marginal conditions many would consider them lethal; how many patient mothers brave the unemployment, the poverty, the

insecurity and desperation in which their families
survive... name a more endurant living creature!
When she scorns her limits, giving her life seems to
this sainted animal the least she can do. Only animals
know bounds, those set by instinct; without instinct,
men pitch their fragile and mobile tent, with neither
solid wall nor protection against the unlimited.

Who knows what the body can do?

Pain

That our weakness betrays us every day, that we
endure a hundred diseases, that we burn in four
minutes with nothing remaining of this peculiar
organization but four pinches of ash, who can
deny it? All the more reason for admiring that this
extreme fragility reaches such high records and can
combat the worst of pains. But, in circumstances
where our descendants take pills, we used to endure
everything; from hominin beginnings up until
yesterday morning, suffering lay in wait at the center of
things, accompanying bodies in their day-to-day life. For
our comfort, we've changed this, so much so that our
children treat their scratches. But refusing pain seems
as dangerous to me as accepting every one of them.
Anesthesia does not win out over dolorism, nor
does the integral drug over universal resignation. All
ideologies, when laying claim to globality, are of equal
worth and worth nothing. What will we have gained

by having a generation of insensitives replace all the flayed who preceded? Like all trials, pain presents two sides, positive and negative: it tortures and comforts, weakens and increases, diminishes the body and knowledge to the point of destruction, ennobles all we've learned and reinvents health. Whatever pity I feel for suffering, including my own, and however unconditionally I seek to assuage it, the fact remains that suffering tests the limits of the body in the same way as does exercise: the latter in an active way, the former, passively. The term *trial* has a single meaning underlying two almost opposed senses: testing and criterion, danger or ordeal. Hence the hesitation: should such putting to the test be encouraged, or should a definitive affliction be rejected? The training that leads the heart to stand up to a marathon or builds up the muscles needed to lift overly heavy dumbbells negotiates these possibilities all the way to the precincts of death; accident and illness do the same. Any given tissue can, in fact, be torn, except at the site of the scar; once past the reaction to the microbe, you can no longer die from it. What does not kill makes stronger, and how can this strength be acquired without running the risk of destruction? Hence the terror that presided over the first vaccinations, when it wasn't known whether they cure or kill. Infectious diseases create antibodies and, in the long run, transform parasites into symbionts. Likewise, I've known one-armed men, table tennis champions, who snatched their paddle from under their armpit, after having tossed the ball for the serve, like lightning; I have thus admired a hundred corporal feats motivated by inferiorities which, conversely, could have produced irreversible disorders. See how far these scales rock: exposing fortifies, protecting weakens, confronting dislocates, assisting soothes. Must we always brave danger? Stupidity. A certain limit can't be passed; intensive training and extraordinary feats exhaust and can kill. Should we, conversely, always advise crutches? Nothing could be less certain. How many hidden heroes do we know of who did valiant relentless battle against cancer, AIDS, continuous daily suffering? Many triumphed over it. Pessimism, a luxury of the old and blasé rich, retreats before optimism, the combat philosophy of the weak when faced with adversity. What do the poor have left, except a heart for fighting? As for myself, I don't regret a single illness, anguish, or misfortune in love. Sensation guides life; pain warns of death. I've lived fully from its deafening howls. So everything is decided at this limit: just how far is too far? Should we, on the pretext of strengthening ourselves, never anesthetize ourselves, do away with all aid and assistance? If yes, the glory of the strong kills the weak and legitimizes the collective crime. If no, then social protection, public health and medicine arise, the long easing of pains via that pity in front of death without which hominity would never have appeared. The optimism of exercise and combat remains true up until its turnaround, quickly withdrawing when it justifies social Darwinism and the exploitation of men by their fellows. So how do we negotiate suffering? Positively and negatively, like violence.

The body survives by turning this double blindness to good account. It doesn't cheat, but remains silent; it tells the truth, but we don't listen to it very well. Its experience prevails over all speculation. *Patior, ergo sum.* I am initially what pain has made of my body; only after, much later and long after, am I what I think. I see what you are suffering and how you manage to endure the pain, I can tell you who you are; what you think rarely confesses, and what you say endlessly lies.

Forgetfulness

However, just as confession is accompanied by insincerity, and thought doubled with the shadow of the unthought, so the body performs certain gestures all the more easily when they unfold from the least amount of attention possible. Of course, the body isn't deceptive, but it's only at ease in a certain obscurity, a tomb of secrets. How freely do we breathe when this function, voluntary or involuntary at will, does without this latter? We run, walk, piss, perform complicated tasks better... while thinking about something else. Ask a skier how he links his turns or a pianist how he performs his virtuoso passages; because they can't explain it, you think they're stupid, while your question, idiotic, shows itself to be completely ignorant of the body: performing its feats faster than lightning, it does without the mind and its supervision; it doesn't like consciousness, and the feeling is mutual. What consciousness stiffens, forgetfulness makes flexible. By dint of self-observation, Narcissus grows stiff in the joints; he becomes mortally melancholic about it. Instruct the clumsy in loss of consciousness.

Learning then drives gestures down into the blackness of the body; thoughts too, besides; knowing is forgetting. Supple virtuality and the passage into act demand a kind of unconsciousness. To inhabit your body better, forget it, at least in part – and to give it orders as well. For the voluntary command of the limbs and even a certain consciousness we have of them imply, at the same time, that we don't command them nor are totally conscious of them. The sensations of the phantom limb show, in return, that we still inhabit it, even if, dead or done away with, forgotten more than any other, we can no longer command it. Aided in this by the sympathetic system, the body requires forgetfulness. I love, for his supple strength and self-effacement, this untiring companion who never pushes himself forward, whereas the permanent arrogance of consciousness and language weighs me down. What a strange collage is this association of the humble with the vain!

Be it physical or moral, pain cries: how to forget this unbearably present body? That usual habitat, in fact, presupposes forgetfulness so that we can live there even more comfortably. Onto this vague background of a quasi-absent body, suffering brings an excess of presence and lucidity. It uproots this blindness, so necessary to our everyday life as well as to our most difficult actions. Pain increases with consciousness and consciousness with pain. What are we lacking when we suffer? The virgin, full of vivacious bodily unconsciousness. This white virginity, this absence of noise and sense, this black box unknowingness, this smooth and even equilibrium, all result, I imagine, from a zero-sum that assembles all the limbs, adding up their singular calls, their partial presences, their particular tints, their obliquities; each of them acts in cooperative concourse with the others to bring about this absent knot. Health boils down to this nullity. Let one of them, in the grips of pain, split off from this cooperative concourse, and it will, dare I say, discourse; I hear it breaking from this zero-sum; a strange force is detaching itself from the balance, dragging the rebirth of the whole along with it; a howling of presence is bursting forth over the new background noise that the entire rest of the body, for lack of equilibrium, is then emitting. The more the limb splits off, the more it shrieks; the more it groans, the more it moves off. I hear the mangled body's moaning. But, since my listening, troubled, can't distinguish between this singular lament and the background noise that surrounds it, the painful place lies at my body's center and in its totality. Then, suffering occupies space. Health made me a mute transparency, an absence, a point without place in the world, a nonego; pain swells it to the point of overrunning the environment. I was a shadow; dense and voluminous, I only exist from pain. Consciousness and the ego, first pathologies, are opposed to health's divine unconsciousness. What is the unconscious? The body. Better: the body in good shape. The most conscious of men was named Narcissus, a word deriving from narcosis: a young man so afflicted that, intoxicated by narcotics, he drowned from an overdose.

Just as he was about to die at the point of Achilles' sword, Hector beseeched him not to mutilate him: what can be said about suffering more profound than those scattered members constantly described in ancient myths and certain Christian legends? Pain causes the body to explode; as Hector proclaims, such separation is more costly than death. When they said that humanity was born from the bones of the Earth sown upon herself, the Greeks made us the children of pain; in order to beget us, they said, the first woman threw stones behind her back... and ever since we've been occupying space with our presence and consciousness, with our limbs and pains. I diminish and divide while limping toward the end; upon which of my last organs will my navigation finish?

EXISTENCE AS DEVIATION FROM EQUILIBRIUM

When standing at the top of a sharp crest beetling over a vertical void, a single impulsion suffices; minuscule, it casts into the abyss; one must walk the straight and narrow. Seated at the bottom of the valley, on the contrary, any force that deviates from this position falls backward, with gravity sufficing to bring whomsoever back to this bottom. Scientists call these two positions: unstable equilibrium, at the top of a circle, and stable, at the bottom; in order to maintain the first, every force must be combined, but the weakest one suffices to destroy it; any force whatsoever restores the second, indestructible. Likewise, the silence of the organs requires muteness from all of them, while the slightest discomfort mixes into transparent health a drop that renders all of it turbid; for the most local pain occupies and recruits the totality of the body, while pleasure, exclusive, requires its complete collaboration, without so much as an irksome speck in the heel of the shoe. Good and evil are like these two situations of equilibrium: to obtain peace, everyone must behave the same; let one individual, aggressive, slander or envy, and he hurls everyone toward war; no one, then, will be able to extricate himself from this hell. As a necessary condition, the good demands unanimous cooperation; while evil merely requires, as sufficient condition, a single individual's least act or even intention. Difficult to the point of unattainability, the one demands an extraordinarily rare maximum, the other an easy minimum. With pain and evil, one individual, tyrannical, lays down the law; the good or pleasure both call for the totality of voices. God is defined then by an omnitude and Satan as an individual. Divine health; diabolic pain.

Yet, mysteriously, the body can, often, thwart these laws of statics. By playing its game off-equilibrium, by confronting its limits... it succeeds in establishing another high seat, in the instability. But if it can construct this new state off-equilibrium from the previous equilibrium, it's conceivable then that life itself from the start became established by means of an initial deviation comparable to this one in every respect. This position, exposed several times over – this secret enveloped within singular existences and life in general – causes the body to leave behind the domain of the real to enter into potential. Yes, the body exists in potency, in every sense imaginable. Without this new self-evidence, how can we understand the progress made in training, the second wind, being in the zone, the explosion of life, adaptation, the contented well-being beyond pain, virtue itself?

ETHICS

Vices: avarice hoards; wrath and pride swell; gluttony stuffs itself or gets drunk; lust collects; envy digs the black hole of its resentment; tired to the point of continual yawning, sloth again seeks rest: without all these resumptions, there would be no pleasure in the deadly sins. Tragically and permanently compliment-deprived, the vain individual seeks them, everywhere, from everyone; the miser, unsatiated, always needs a penny to round off a pound and top off his leaky strong box; swollen with ire, the furious individual asks every situation for reasons to rage; the alcoholic and the greedy pig have forever lost satiety; under his heading, the lecher lays out a thousand and three women, and more besides, if he can; every detail assures the jealous individual in his hatred; the idler wears himself out on his obligatory bed... never filled, swept up in the spiral that imprisons them, the seven vicious individuals of the canon all suffer from a single ill: growth. Each of them bears within an infinite pit that an intolerable anesthesia obliges him to fill: he must, once more and at fresh cost, re-stimulate lack of appetite, re-liven blasé insensibility, reheat coldness. Vice recaptures the vicious in its spiral.

Through lack of understanding virtue, the collection of vices takes on a nice coherent unity: an entire life devotes itself to inflation, to the enlargement of an expanding mass. This growth develops according to a narcotic-looking slope: the miser, idler and glutton drug themselves with sleep, alcohol or money; the dose of rage, hatred or fame must be increased in order to remain enchanted for very long with wrath, envy or pride. Why don't we speak of virtue any more? Because the world in which we live is built, precisely, upon growth, general and quantifiable; the economy, finance, consumption and the innovative progress of science and technology, everything that appears serious and heavy, seem to make growth as necessary as fate, as indispensable as addiction. As a result, our culture itself can scarcely be distinguished from a growing narcosis that enslaves to its dependency. Why do children drug themselves? To imitate their parents, intoxicated with money, work, schedules, consumption, social roles... subject to obligatory hourly doses, deeply under the spell of growth. Have young generations ever obeyed more submissively?

We discourse more easily on vices because their true nature, entirely intellectual, is easier to understand. The head is constantly doing their calculations:

the gray and simplistic arithmetic of pleasures, doses, women conquered, amassed treasures, the buzzing volume of renown, the compared blows that struck home on the opponent, the hours spent doing nothing.... Nothing in all this has to do with the body; everything in it, on the contrary, refers to numbers: the vices, intellectual, invite discourse. We drug ourselves above all with numbers and language. Conversely, stemming from the body, that is to say from the heart, moral worth comes from courage: from the recognition and refusal of our finitude. The first and only virtue that matters and the one from which the others are deduced, courage turns its back on reason as much as invention scoffs at criticism. By nature corporal, cordial, cardiac, courage, essential and primary, is as difficult to understand as the élan vital: without reflection or long meditation, its generosity immediately finds concord and its fidelity *misericordia*.... So to discover virtue, one must penetrate down to life's very roots, down to energy's primary biochemical reactions or time's basic rhythms; there, courage in its principle is born to the secret of its effectiveness and the inchoative expression of its forces. In the metabolism's heat or the élan vital's surging, with the heart's elementary beating... it is from here that courage leaps, a total and warm forgetting of self toward the world, others, the neighbor and objects. At the moment of birth, from the open doorway of time between the parturient woman's legs, a gushing torrent bursts forth, a flood of non-being, a warm and vital geyser, a treasure of potential, a savage cry, a first hoarse expiration, capable of warming the outside world. The virtue of vitality imparts life, plus love.

By what miracle of life does courage scoff at death, provoke it to its very face, defy it in the nether realm of its law? The heart pulls us where we refuse, with all our judgment, to go. This virtue scoffs at good sense, the same way the body knows how to go beyond the head, no matter what it may think about it. Death alone grounds our humanity, therefore all our moralities, the vices and the virtue; courage in the face of the Reaper marks out our limits and opens our aspirations toward the unlimited; the hominin animal, good, knows but ignores that it dies. The body constructs its deviations from equilibrium by courage or by heart.

THE VIRTUAL BODY; RIGHT, POLITICS

It beats, my ribs heave, my heels strike the ground, my hair flutters with the movement. But the whole of life, too, moves: for plants grow and their *fertilisine* takes flight, algae float and mushrooms spread, but less than bacteria do. Furthermore, life doesn't merely change place, it changes. Viviparous animals transform during the course of embryogenesis, certain insects go from pupa to imago, organisms grow and develop, degenerate and die, rot and decompose, returning finally to the primitive molecules that are restored to the universal stock. Life doesn't merely move and change, it exchanges: by means of the metabolism and the diverse transactions negotiated with its environment, life fights against disorder. These commonplaces, though necessary for the definition of life, aren't sufficient to account for another dimension. Our body exchanges, moves, of course; it changes, indeed. But not always according to a plan, nor along linear time, nor to defend itself from the growing entropy – either in movement or throughout its development or against degeneration. For humanity's transformations sometimes take unexpected paths genetics doesn't foresee, no doubt: I could have been a pianist and played scales all the day long, but here I am a watchmaker having to mend tiny wheelworks. A certain tennis player misses soccer. Abandoning one group of forms, my body adopts another. Its metamorphoses distinguish it from other living things. Here, the body varies in quite a new way. It would be better, in fact, to give this process – unforeseen by the life sciences – a new name. Bacteria, mushrooms, plants or animals, human included, live by metabolism; mankind is distinguished from them by its metamorphism. In addition to exchanges at every scale, the former adopt positions but can't multiply them at will, while we gesticulate infinitely and pull faces. Coming home from a run and playing tennis, here then is that other, a surgeon with a passion for horses; this morning, he enters into an angry scene and this evening will stroke his children's heads.... How do we define a body given over to so many poses and signs: when and under which form is it itself? How do we get beyond so many differences according to the person: when and under which form is it us? These multiple postures prevent us from saying. My body and our species don't exist so much in concrete reality as "in potency" or virtuality.

Philosophies and political theories frequently exhaust themselves trying to define freedom, because in their descriptions and determinations constraint or necessity always reappears like a disquieting and contradictory twin. To free oneself from this labyrinth, it's enough to start from the body and its singular life. Then, all power must, in every circumstance, stop short of the body's integrity; with hands free and plenty of elbow room, it has the right to move as it pleases; it must be able to control its own nature, and therefore its capability. Its virtuality is thus opposed to all power. Freedom is defined by the body and the body by potential.

THE TWO METAMORPHOSES

Fables, stories in which all living things give signs, teach profound things. La Fontaine began his last book with "The Companions of Ulysses"; metamorphosed into animals, these companions decline to become human again, confessing thereby that they have finally found their definitive point of equilibrium, their true character, their fundamental passion. This is how and why men can become animals, why their respective bodies imitate a species, and how fables are written. Fairy tales fascinate children because, endowed with a hundred degrees of freedom, their bodies lend themselves, as much as those of gymnasts and dancers, to every possible transformation, and because this capability, almost infinitely supple, lets them understand from within, by a delighted coenesthesia, the workings of the magic wand, which are less illusory than virtual, less inspired by sorcery than a pedagogy of the possible. Ulysses' sailors have lost this.

Who is hiding behind Merlin, the magician? The body itself: at will, it becomes the fairy Carabosse, Donkey Skin and carriage, Beauty and Beast, the little mermaid with her scale-wrapped hips, lamb and wolf, Akela and Baloo, Bagheera the panther, Bororo and Arara, the frog who wanted to be as big as the ox, field rat and city rat, god, table, basin, and, in sum, multiform Proteus.... The powerful spell of fables, fairy tales, dance and fetishes emanates from these multiple simulations. We no longer believe in such legends, because we've forgotten the enchanting body and the extraordinary blossoming of its forms. Let's summon, here, to the child's side, male and female dancers, athletes and gymnasts, hunters and fishermen, people of all trades who work with their hands, the deaf and the mute, the timid and the uneducated, in brief, the throng of all those who philosophy, ever since it took the floor, has cut off from speaking. This first metamorphosis transforms the body as much as the body wants and can: and it can do many things that astonish the mind.

In the second metamorphosis, conversely, the animated process of simulation is checked by the aging that, then, changes each of us into a species: specialized, totemized, stuffed and preserved, according to one's destiny, the passions of one's character, the imbecility of one's corporatism or one's vices: envy, resentment, cramped avarice, stupidity, gluttony and boastfulness... here one is, a polished insect in its chitin, a little gray mouse, a silly goose, sated hog with bristly hide, tom turkey pleased with itself, cruel shark, cowardly vulture, crawling reptile... through the first metamorphosis, a certain youthfulness passed through every species, since *Homo sapiens*, by mimicking them, summarized them, but the checking of the vital flow has statufied him, as though aged, into a particular animal. At work our entire lives, death occasions our fall into a genus, into the specialty of a corporation, by impelling us toward membership, whose devouring passion hardens our habits, freezes our gestures, prefers the dryness of bones to supple flesh and soft skin: this is why we represent it with the aid of a skeleton. It transforms us into a wooden framework, whereas life continuously opens up choice. Fighting against the stiffenings of age requires that the individual – should that individual wish to remain one – refuse the comfort of inhabiting his category, that he resist therefore that second metamorphosis, by opposing to speciation, creaking with scales and leather, the suppleness of his velvety singularity, or better, that he stay available for any possible simulation, on condition that it remain reversible: the individual agreed to become a fish, this morning, in order to slip between the piers of the bridge, with fast waters, but he must be able, this evening, to become a fox again, when researching and thinking, or a grasshopper, if dancing. So then, my soul, read fables. The body unfolds these virtualities before the soul and teaches them.

UNDERSTANDING

As reptile or mole, I lie hidden in holes, dark and cold, already a cadaver, but also the humid humus and dry rock of the burrow or sap where the roots of the tree that I am as well rejoins them, but also grass and mouse, bark and bull, bee and gladiolus; as gudgeon or lamprey, I swim through the fleeing waters of rivers; shad or salmon, I head upriver toward headwaters or descend to the sea, but, undulating, I accompany the waters with my viscous locks of green algae, along the riverbed, and with my fluids, I move toward their roiling confluences; as aerial turbulence and shifting breezes, I bear up eagles and vultures, but, during times of intelligence, I soar, high, on my pairs of wings, swallow or lark, or, kestrel, I flutter in place, watchful for some prey, below, to seize in my talons; fire of God, tongue of flame, spirit of fire, flaming branch and salamander, I blaze from my birth on, until a small heap of ashes, wet and heavy, melts into the rock and *boulbènes*, nourishing the earthworms or, vanishing – light, elementary, flying – with the ocean tides or the transparent sheets of wind. Immobile like flora, animated and fauna, primordial as element, finite and feet planted in a place, thorax extended to the horizon, head cloud and light, neurons flying through the vast universe, from the mountain to the stars, pores shivering next to the fireplace; contracted, dilated, dense and rare, dissolved, liquid and forged by the hammer and furnace of metamorphosis, I am nothing other than the other things, plus the other men in the world. Then and then only, do I understand.

For, likewise, I become, for better or for worse, the dregs and saintliness of those close to me, and, by patient extension, the crime and goodness of those most distant, at the extreme edge of cultures; I don't mimic them so much as I absorb them, digest them, incorporate them, so that an old quadroon becomes, in me, an octoroon. The other makes my flesh, their flesh blended with mine: this, this thing right here, haunts my body, and this animal too, but this one, the other, above all, enters into my body, one so mixed, so crossbred and penetrated that, lost in the very middle of that great crowd that effaces me, I vanish like a bit of vapor. This is the secret of the ancient totemisms: the seagull patrol makes fun of the antelope patrol, and the bulls challenge, in the stadium, the blue jays.... But I seem to understand you better, when I begin with your passions, your tigress anger, your earth idleness, your mountain pride, your coleopteran avarice, your reptilian tenderness, your she-ass lascivity, and if I show you my burning and my sequoia slowness, you will understand me, so much easier does it become to reach one another through our four basic natures – mineral, vegetable, animal and world. We-things build the road to us others, we-animals blaze the trail toward the soon-to-be intelligent us.... I love you, sometimes, the way a dog does his bitch, by pure sense of smell, the way an octopus undulates its eight arms, the way a tree entwines its branches with the wind.

Metamorphoses of the enamored body: universal love passes through sand, floral games and animal races; those in love begin this way, with the desire for things and the world, before crowning one another in corporal ecstasy in God. We will only understand one another when we join together in the round or in the dance of all these melanges.

Producing

Required by the task of the work, attention produces an ecstatic exit from oneself that's so total and radical it turns, at will, the attention-giver into that toward which attention is focusing its patient intention: here he is as Hermes, caduceus in hand, playing the messenger; blind, loyal, in love, he races across Siberia to save the Czar's brother's neck; Harlequin, he sees in his mirror the image of an old half-breed, quadroon or octoroon; flies and sings like an Angel; motionless like Atlas, he gets around like Hercules... but no, he doesn't transform into man or woman, into animal or Archangel, only, but also into thing and stone, dead body or statue, fire and mist, river and turbulence, atom or crystal, relief or fragrance, ocean or wind, chart... how can one not know where the Gulf Stream flows, when one is the Gulf Stream? Attention casts the so-called first person into the object, animal or man – the third person – in such a way that I possess, direct and inhabit that third person in the sense whereby a demon haunts it, or rather and better, it casts itself into me in such a manner that it possesses, directs and inhabits me in the sense whereby its devil haunts me... no, I no longer know whether I am it or it is me: how better than by means of this confusion or confluence, this quasi-chemical reaction, this subtle phase transition, to know anything? In any event, the attention-giver knows. Without this mixture, without simulation and the metamorphoses produced by it, there is no knowledge or science.

The work asks the body to turn into a tree: from a certain arm or branching, Hermes would blossom, sitting astride, the Parasite would fructify on others, like our druid's mistletoe, while on others still, the Harlequin and Half-breed would undress themselves, whilst on the topmost branch the Angels would sing and at the foot of the trunk, stiff, the Statues would sit enthroned, while at the top of the canopy the clamors, colors, odors, caresses and delights of the Five Senses would rustle, like foliage... this is a flora with a strange fauna, or, rather, for the fire that flows through the body, a fluvial arborescence whose tributaries, Lot and Gers, Tarn and Baise... should have furnished the titles of my books, a fluviatile network distributing streams of sap to the main trunk. What is an author, if not this tree-shaped body? Good ones bear or shelter thousands of characters, teem with life, fire and fertility, for inventiveness persists through time, spreads out in the eight directions of space, in a gushing foliage of supple branches, mobile in the turbulent locks of the wind, attentive to capturing the circulations, tenuous and universal, of warmth, of mother waters, of intuitive fertilisine, in order to reproduce them as a leafy population of catkins, fruits, nests, songs and playhouses for children. What then is an author, if not this life-producing body? In natural history, the tree is no mere plant genus; it bears the five kingdoms and all the families.

But this flood of terms and images remains empty and this book incomplete, because a male is writing it. Women alone know what the body can do: produce another body, one resembling her own and different from it. Since I've had no experience of the stunning process by which a mother's womb multiplies an egg into thousands of billions of diverse and ordered cells, what do I, in truth, know of production? Nothing worth mentioning; I should have stepped aside. The male body speaks through the wind; fertile, heavy, real, the female conceives, carries, delivers, nurses; her body lives at least twice. The word flies, flesh produces.

THE TRANSFIGURATION

In the silence of health, the body – absorbed in its capacity for omnitude – knows nothing of membership. Illness causes it to fall into a description.

Only syndromes exist, the healthy don't say a word. Thus, we aptly say the physically fit body, in the singular: it can, then, do anything, that is, produce a thousand possible metamorphoses. The omnivalent substratum for all these transformations, the transcendental personal body, thus, becomes white. Virtual, therefore white. White blazon of the human body: the sum of the colors it can assume, the set of clothes the bony framework can wear. White: as intelligent as the understanding; white: as transparent as the soul; white: universal.

Matthew 17:1-8: "on a high mountain apart, he was, then, transfigured in front of them; his face shone like the sun and his clothes became as white as light...." A theology of the body, Christianity venerates it in the Incarnation, communes with it via the Eucharist and resurrects it, lastly, glorious; not only after death, but during the entirety of life, the body enters into glory. The Son of God and Man becomes incarnate in a woman's womb, leaving his body and blood in memory. The mystery of the Incarnation expresses the fact that we don't know what the flesh is or can do, because it participates in divinity; it signifies that the flesh conceals a mystery, something Spinoza repeats. Jesus Christ speaks more often of his body than of his soul: the soul is that bodily glory or joy that Christianity announces after death. More virtual than actual, the glorious body is the real body; I have seen, transfigured, faces shining as brilliantly as suns and skins white as snow. The Transfiguration sets out the incandescence of possibilities and the omnitude of metamorphoses.

Other Passages to Potential

And yet the black hollow, the well of potential in which at night the body, while gently slipping into the unconsciousness of sleep, becomes invaginated, isn't this where the body is going to draw the recovery of its forces for tomorrow's continuous bouquet of gestures and movements? Abandoned, back stretched out and muscles relaxed, blind and silent, mouth half open and eyes closed, defenselessly delivered over, arms arching around the head, breathing reduced and regular... here is another sought after non-posture: unknowing, white, re-posed or pre-posed, universal, from which, by waking, the body will be poured, in several hours, into the chain of real gestures, of defense and capture. The night and the siesta bring it back to virtuality. Does it, when sometimes curled up in the fetal position, take up again its other white prehistory, by repeating in its sleep the intrauterine ecstasy and, through waking, its birth? Reversing the passage into act, falling asleep passes into potential. We often know what we're doing when, wide-awake, we take up trowel or spade to tackle digging or building, but do you know what you're doing when you're falling asleep? You are, precisely, abandoning all act so as to pour toward the viscosity of the virtual: less passive than potential. Every gesture, every discrete sequence of positions would be an obstacle to this strange skidding along a rock slab over which one falls all the better for neglecting to follow it. If the body's existence is deciphered on its wide-awake pantomimes, sleep, black with night, white with potential, envelops its essence. Which of the two precedes the other in the lunar round of days?

White Hair

Here I am then, having arrived at the age whose weight I could see on the shoulders of the old men when I was a child. Could it be that they were carrying within themselves, as I feel I do in my body today, the same laughing little boy, joyous and youthful, under their wrinkles and inside the arched curve of their backs? Just as a number reckons the years, this same number also gauges the interval between this flexibly fidgeting boisterer and the stiff joints that remain of him and which form — how well I know it — the comet's tail of this brilliant nucleus, ever-present within. Am I to believe that, back then, my grandparents loved, in me, a living reproduction of the tiny Russian doll which, in their hearts, was beating time and whose permanence was protected by the tabernacle of their breath, since tears immediately come to me as soon

as I see, outside me, those just starting lives laugh and
run, those lives that correspond so precisely to he
who, in my chest, has never stopped loving, hoping
or dancing?

How many tents, in addition, are fitted in me,
tents whose skin walls shelter, as well, the planning
adolescent and the throng of adults regretful of the
immense joys so late in coming? For the number
of years reckons, also, one by one, those persons,
multiple, who take up residence under senility's
worn-out appearance. Don't think they necessarily
get along well with one another, under the pretext
that they stated, successively, the same first and last
name as mine, for they don't always speak the same
language: the youngest chatters Gascon and the
oldest stammers out English, one, among the earliest
inhabitants, only thinks about fishing and breaking
the rocks of the Garonne and another only about
holding the ship's course to leeward of Guernsey, the
atheist turns his back on the one who prays, the athlete
is amazed at the monk, the silent solitary mocks the
lecturer, the contemplative allows the entrepreneur
to go about his business and the mystic, strangely,
gets along, a twin, with the one in love. Whom are
you addressing?

The one called I and me and you and he, depending,
acts as the switchboard operator who connects,
quickly, Paris with Chile, to let the American converse

with the Japanese. The stilted clumsiness of old age stems from the fact that it, often, becomes confused among the thousands of plugs and connections, but its deft flexibility stems from the fact that it shares the same roof with all these people, indoors, so that all the outside, so alike, comes to it almost naturally. Whoever you may be, or almost, I am too. Thus old age sees youth, conversely, as all alone and starchy. Sole, the youth; so numerous, the old man; the green vitality of youth is of one color, whereas ancientness spreads its rainbow fan. But, amid the spectrum, emerald still shines. Our body fills with virtualities.

But here I am also, having arrived at the moment and threshold where I enjoy darkness more than every color and night above every light; where I prefer silence to every music, voice and murmur; where solitude weighs so lightly on me I seek it out and cultivate it; where that multi-colored mob recedes to the point of disappearing, like a tide; where the sky, intense or gray, the sea, divine and wine-dark, the desert, ocher and celestial, the glacier whose lucidity is blind to the green crevasses, the flat prairie, a never-ending paradise, nourish and enchant me more than any interesting story. I am leaving difference so as to love infinity.

No doubt, all these people and all these doubles are but one and the same; no doubt, the internal and the external fuse to merge into a single variety: they are all me, I am all men who are but one, who are the world and the world absorbs me; as for the colored spectrum, it translates the white light in another manner, distracting from this intuitive luminosity with a science whose every detail shimmers and rustles, glistens and gleams, multiplies into useless echoes, whose analyses prattle, fatigue and don't make us live. The more I draw nigh monotonous meadows, walk in mystic and limitless deserts, dive into the smooth ocean or the unfading sky, reach blinding glaciers... the better I live, rejuvenated, at the primary and tranquil wellspring where two, several and one have not yet burst forth into their bouquet. Is eternity reckoned by this punctual circle?

Knowledge

First figures: in 1749, in the eighth chapter of his *Natural History of Man*, entitled "On the Senses in General," Buffon recounted how the first human discovered his senses and, from touch alone, the external world. To the list of the figures of the primitive ancestor drawn by myths and philosophies in those times, five heroes of the senses are added: in his *Treatise on the Sensations* from 1754, Condillac described a statue that smelled like a rose, whose stony body arising from fragrant effluvia plagiarized Buffon's Adam; likewise, Molyneux's congenitally blind man, operated on, began to see, and the Abbot de l'Épée enabled the deaf-mute to converse by signs. The *Meno's* ignorant ancient slave boy who knew, without having learned it, geometry is joined by Victor, the Wild Boy of Aveyron, passing, dumbfounded, from nature to culture. The question concerning the origin of knowledge presents characters in stories in which experiences often remain in a state of virtuality.

For the infant has, from birth, neither a complete sense of smell nor touch, since myelinisation only advances with the weeks. The five senses progress slowly. During this time, the infant acquires the motivity of gestures; does he mimic before his senses are formed, by means of his postures? Does he see the model before imitating it? Or does he imitate it in order to see it better?

From the Five Senses to Culture

Not long ago, in *The Five Senses*, I recognized the inadequacy of the sensualism professed by the Enlightenment to account for the origin of knowledge; there is nothing in the understanding, it repeated after the tradition, which has not first been in the senses: *nihil est in intellectu quid non prius fuerit in sensu*. Yet, at the end of the path that began with sensation, sapience gives way to sagacity; I mean by this that, better than leading to that knowledge which is canonized by science, this path leads, in fact, to a refined sense of taste, bestows an exquisite sense of smell and a velvety sense of touch, forms a discerning sense of sight for nuance, cultivates a musical sense of hearing or subtle linguistics... in brief, fashions a discriminating cultivation or initiates into one of the fine arts. Even then such blossoming remains rare: how many around us make good use of their skin, their eardrums, their taste buds; how few complain about the ugliness and the noise that pollute space, about the horror of massacred landscapes, about the stinking cities, about a food extolled for its rapidity rather than its sapidity? What remains, finally, of sensory knowledge in abstraction, libraries, screens and networks? Never has anyone seen the detailed path from the color blue to the word *blue* that no longer has anything blue about it, from senses to concept; biochemical receptors and intersynaptic messengers have never led to a thought unscathed by protein and electric charge. Sensory refinement induces a high culture, this is the fair result of experience: the aesthetic ends in aesthetics, the *sapiens* of wisdom is descended from that of sapidity. Does sensualism amount to an academic quirk?

This path from the senses toward understanding, on the other hand, makes the rest of the body vanish or, rather, reduces it to the function of a conveyance for the five peripheral terminals: is such a physiology necessary for the simple walker? The old sensualism, but also the cognitive sciences and logical empiricism, propose a genesis of knowledge that would be bodiless. In order that it should carry the sense of smell, Condillac sculpts the body as a statue: dead and frozen, scarcely veined, marble replaces the supple, multiple, fervent and animated flesh. Why detest it to the point of making it into a funerary slab or a stone lighthouse?

Imitation as Origin of Knowledge

This, on the other hand, is what I want to show: that there is nothing in knowledge which has not been first in the entire body, whose gestural metamorphoses, mobile postures, very evolution imitate all that surrounds it. Our knowledge arises from others who learn it from ours, which, by teaching it thus, remembers it and by exposing it, augments it, in indefinite cycles of positive growth, which nonetheless are sometimes blocked by the stupidity of obedience. Gestural as much as receptive – thus more active than passive – osseous, muscular, cardiovascular, neural... bearer, certainly, of the five senses, but with other functions than channeling exterior information toward a central processor, the body recovers in this way a cognitive presence and function of its own, eliminated by the couple sense-understanding, whereas imitation, on the contrary, implies sensory activity.

The origin of knowledge resides in the body, not only intersubjective but also objective knowledge. We don't know anyone or anything until the body takes on its form, its appearance, its movement, its *habitus*, until the body joins in a dance with its demeanor. Thus, the corporal schema is acquired and exposed, is stored in a quick and forgetful memory, is improved and refined. Receiving, emitting, retaining, transmitting: all actions of the expert body. Afterwards, imitation will engender reproduction, representation and virtual experience, terms consecrated by the sciences, the arts and computer simulation technologies. The new recording media for the memorization and transport of signs, like wax tablets, parchment and the printing press, have made us forget the body's priority in these functions; cultures without writing know them still.

But while imitation implies the activity of the senses, it often subdues it. When rivalry – imitation in the negative – has them in its grips, the hunter can approach the wildest of beasts: thus in Yellowstone National Park, I managed to touch elk, formerly unapproachable, with my hand, when springtime was driving them to fight other males amongst the females in heat, or Parisian intellectuals in political debate. Imitation, rapid, renders a more than slow flesh blasé; all-powerful, mimicry freezes sensorial sensitivity or renders it frigid. When they don't lead to cultural refinement, and they rarely do, or mastery, extremely rare, of one of the fine arts, the senses ordinarily serve to monitor and verify mimetic accuracy. Concurrent, they converge toward gestures.

Let's set out now, by the new path, from what everyone knows to what I'm proposing: from learning to the invention of the sciences. From early infancy, the face mimics grimaces, the mouth emits like gurglings, with gestures completing the symmetries. The face is sculpted by those around it. How do we learn emotions and mental states, if not by recognizing them in others? How do we recognize them without experiencing them? Experience them without imitating them? Learn them without mimicking them? Mimic them without learning them? This repeated circle grows and makes us grow.

Whether they love each other or hate each other, two individuals face to face weigh their bodies in a cycle of this kind. The collectivity, far from precluding the gestures of love, on the contrary, induces into them; among so many hateful, hostile, cold bodies, how many would have any idea of tenderness if the mirror of their peers didn't invite them to it, to the point of obligation? Passion is born of these face-to-faces, tête-à-têtes, vis-à-vis and hand to hands, the major process of acquisition and growth. Speech is acquired as a muscular and neural echo; the muscular finesse required for speech reaches the muscles recruited for writing. Why precisely those? Face, mouth and hands imitate in a mobile, expressive and skillful manner: Echo and Narcissus rise from the most innervated places of the homunculus. Did this latter acquire this select innervation by dint of theater?

We do, of course, learn the figures of ballerinas, the gestures of gymnasts and the practices of the trades, but it would be better to say that everything is acquired, precisely, through dance and the mirror, through sports and tricks of the trade, through the mother and child's tête-à-tête (where the daughter or son teaches the adult as much as she does them), through the warriors' mano a mano, the professor and student's as well as the boss and employee's vis-à-vis, the lovers' reciprocal prayer... all of society in pas de deux. Nothing is more effective for education than the theater's face-to-face. All individual sports are played hand to hand: wrestling and sumo strip their combatants, with each confronting the other barehanded. In team sports, soccer, rugby, basketball... a mobile boundary is seen to float between the teams, upfield or offside, and an intermediary object to appear, a ball... a quasi-object which traces out relations and heralds things.

In this description, the violent lexicon, encountered in its natural state, shows how opposition mimics best and how conversely imitation quickly turns into conflict: when you oppose, you copy. Does love hold up between lovers a more tarnished mirror than hatred with its shining surface? Does Jacob become an angelic prophet from having spent the night fighting the Archangel? Does the disciple stop putting the master to death? What is going on in classrooms and theaters, where the instructor and actor, hated as much as loved, occupy the dubious position of the victimary king, having to deploy the seductions of language and gesture in order to evade aggression? Attempt to mimic someone truly, and with the utmost fidelity; then you draw near, but so near you suddenly find yourself taking the very place of the person you were copying: you evict him... hence war and violence. That being so, if the origin of accurate knowledge resides in this exact imitation, conflict will always accompany it. The body's gymnastic exercises, begun in the grimace and dance, continue on as aggressive melee, while theatrical representation continues on as tragedy, as comedy where the ridiculous dies: war, mother of things and men. Love and hate mingle in learning: Empedocles, the first theorist of these two uniting and separating elements, completes Heraclitus, the first philosopher of dark battle. We are continually following in the footsteps, recognizable in our sciences, of this identifiable origin, from the atomic bomb to the risks incurred by life and the environment. The anthropological origin of knowledge is formed in a simulation that's so close that love and hate mix with and imitate one another in it, that imitation mixes love with hate in it, that hate imitates love in it so as to be mixed with it, and where, finally, love hates imitation: these are the ropes of the originary knot and the secret of its unraveling.

Lived and said in the conditional, play, likewise, places itself in possible positions, imaginary certainly, meaning still virtual, but for which the entire body responds with actual schemata. Like sports, play programs the body by means of imitations and oppositions; trying out software, it stores them in memory. Nothing but what is well known thus far.

The Order: Taking, Learning, Understanding

The accepted theories on the learning process distinguish between objectivist, constructivist, collaborativist, cognitive, and sociocultural models, according to whether they believe in an objective knowledge that's independent of all education, whether they make the learner participate in the construction, non-given, of this knowledge, whether they invite a collective to work for it in common, whether they take into account the learners' aptitudes or their cultural membership. In all these systems, learning presupposes, in accordance with the dogma that one cannot learn what one does not understand, a clear comprehension of what is taught. All acquired knowledge implies an explication.

By this line of reasoning, we wouldn't know very much – except education's grandiose failures in every country where this foolishness prevails. Had it been, indeed, necessary for me to understand everything that I learned at the very moment that I learned it, I would hardly have mastered addition, the singular and the plural, plus the confluence of the rivers opposite which my family lived. What do we truly mean by number at the local grade school? As simple as it is, this concept presents so many difficulties that the best mathematicians are still breaking their teeth trying to crack this nut. In fact, we learn immensely more things than those we master, and understand poorly those that are explained to us just as poorly. A certain memory takes charge of the remaining mass and some unknown corporal agency digests it a good long while. I understood past the age of forty what I had learned by heart at age six and would have understood nothing at all had I not first learned without understanding, had I not taken the lesson just as it was. Does the arrogant overvaluation of clarity derive from the Enlightenment and from a rationalism anxious to chase away the darkness? The gesture of exclusion manifestly grips us like a habit. As much as I esteem, to the point of intoxication, transparency in exposition, I see just as much that we ceaselessly learn the opaque, whose obscurity is no obstacle to retention. We absorb as much of shadow as we do of lights, and knowledge holds fast, in sum, in constant labor at the limits of this chiaroscuro. We rarely know that we don't know and what we do know: two high feats of intelligence; the most often, we know what we don't know, and we know poorly what we do know. We overvalue a lucid cogito, one that is as rare as Newton's sudden illumination in the midst of his apple orchard or that of Descartes in his stove-warmed room. This is how we teach our children, considering them to be like these two geniuses taken at two privileged moments of their inventive life. Is it surprising that education fails? Modesty counsels keeping the patience of the dawn, when the last streaks of night mingle with the break of day. Knowledge does not begin at noon.

The real subject of this mixture of light and shadow, the body remembers and forgets, it is capable of more or less what it believes itself capable, does better or worse than it knows it can do, does not know and knows at the same time, a black box sometimes partially open. Happily, I've learned many things by heart, that wonderful expression, whereby people show things can be learned in such a way that they do not yet rise back up to the brain; my body chewed it over and made it its own, without my knowing it. How many times have I awoken exclaiming: "So that's what

'The Wolf and the Lamb' or some theorem by Cauchy meant!" I finally understood, twenty years later. In sum, comprehension depends less on the explanation given at the time of learning than it changes, evolves, disappears, returns, dies or blossoms. This holds even for mathematics, that double excellence of translucent reason and education: taking, learning, understanding, this is the order of the acquisition of knowledge; reverse it and you'll remain at a standstill, for clarity projects, from the first numbers themselves, an infinite shadow or reveals an infinite depth. Go, run, faith will come to you, the body will sort things out. Knowledge sinks into it and from it re-emerges. Hidden in the shadow, the body slowly assimilates the simulated.

THE BODY'S MEMORY,
AS WELL AS THE WORLD'S AND LIFE'S

Gestures don't need to be repeated very many times for the body to make them its own and become a dancer or a cobbler. Complicated chains of postures are so readily incorporated into its muscles, bones and joints that it buries the memory of this complexity in simple forgetfulness. Afterward, almost without knowing it, the body reproduces these sequences of positions faster than it assimilated them; it imitates, stores and remembers. Who counts the enormous treasure of poses it bears? In incarnated memories, in data become programs, therein lies our primary cognitive base. The more this expanded capital, this unconscious reservoir – for the unconscious is the body – increases, the less it weighs, light, aerial with successful adaptations. What could be more precious than these maps of places visited, housed deep in the corporal memory? So precious that when questioned about the positions of his fellow diners at the banquet after the earthquake that leveled his host's home, Simonides was able to answer and pick out the identity of the people crushed by the ceiling, because the recumbent body immediately sees once again just who is stretched out on the couch to its right and left, in front and nearby, as though the layout of the table were retained in its limbs. No, the body does not aid in the work of a memory lodged elsewhere, it does this work itself, copier and data bank. So precious, moreover, that in the history of every culture, there is no work more widespread than that of copying, from the mural painters of Lascaux, the Assyrian scribes, the monks of the Middle Ages up to Jean-Jacques, transcriber of music; so reflect before laughing at Bouvard and Pécuchet, who having arrived at the end of all knowledge pronounce the ultimate virtue of copyists. But the body knows how to do this work above all else: it mimics things then directly.

For objects themselves imitate one another and mutually copy each other. Stones trace on the ice the sentences of a writing that has no need for us; in memory of its slow advance, the glacier leaves on the mountain giant moraines and steep-sided valleys; fire leaves in the ashes the marks of its ravage; at the bottom of the valley, the thalweg immobilizes the course of the river; on the Indian Ocean, a hotspot vertically marks a long track running from the Deccan Traps to Reunion's volcano, passing through a string of islands; similarly, in the Pacific, in the Galapagos and Hawaii; the ebbing tide writes lines of music in sandy pleats on the foreshore; thus the gust of wind composes on the mobile sea surge and the heat on the till recently tranquil air.... Yes, the elements imitate one another, conserving in their possession the memory of things, neighboring and distant. The names for various conservatories: for ancient magnetism, the rock; for the torrent, the valley; for the eruption, the atoll; for the scorching front, the hurricane... time is graven on space. The world's body plays the role of memory.

Thus, magpies don't beget cuckoos; on the Jaguar's coat an invariant message can be read, one different from that imprinted on the fur of the wolf; through imitation and copying within a species, individuals keep its special memory stable. However different their bodies may appear, the general form of their genus is unmistakably recognizable. Genetics, in order to understand such conservation, deciphers the mechanism of transcriptions, codings and biochemical replications. Formerly confined to the art of traveling painters, natural history turned biology takes up again this art of copying, but after a different manner, by reading it in the windings of DNA. Like the body and the world, life appears as an immense memory whose reserves are exploited by today's technological revolution, just as the preceding one did coal mines. In it, time becomes stabilized on folded ribbons of space; space is cut up and interlockings are carried out in it as though each protein counter-imitated the one to which it fits; matter itself has these universal properties of life and the body. In the objects of the world as well as in living creatures, a manner of knowing resembling our corporal postures – full of life and plunged into things – is revealed, a manner our arts will try to resemble. Positions, first alphabets: Diderot called these bearings and attitudes hieroglyphs.

Lazy or parasitic, we make things and living creatures do, in our stead, what they can do better than us. The graphite of the pencil leaves its trace on the page just as the burnt torch marks the cavern walls with its stroke of inspiration. Could photographs be taken without the effect produced by the bombardment of certain particles on a particular chemical compound? Arts and technologies are only successful when based on properties adapted from inert objects and animated beings. We don't so much imitate them as imitate their manner of imitating, we copy their fashion of copying; we don't so much use them to remember as utilize their memory as memory. Technologies resemble mimicries of mimicries, the chain of which runs from things to the body and from there to our new recording media.

Prior to any technology for the storage and transport of signs, the body remains the primary recording medium for memory and transmission: archaic screen or parchment, we no longer know how to read the body the way our friends without writing can, our friends who make use of it the way our ancestors did wax or ourselves paper. Should I master this reading, I'd be able to decipher upon your wrinkles, like an open book, your history and its tribulations, upon your dance, your desire, and upon the masks and statues of your culture, the encyclopedia of its discoveries. We've lost the medium-body.

Six Heroes

Why then does Harlequin dress in fabrics that are mixed, speckled, mottled, striped...? From having imitated everyone and his masters, he has taken on their forms and colors. The thickness, in depth, of his clothes and the superficial mosaic of his cloak give some idea of the immense corporal memory.

Conversely, Pierrot's white lets its light transparency be seen. When he undresses, Harlequin remembers, by recreating them, the gestures (of persons, in the sense of masks or disguises) stored by the corporal schema. Always still dressed, never naked, he can't get to the bottom of his memory, down to the total and first oblivion. But when Archimedes surged naked from the bath in which he discovered the force that makes us float, he inverts Harlequin, overdressed, the way invention is opposed to memory.

The slavery which set him traveling through the entire body social and taught him, a serf, to counsel princes; the successive sales and his various masters, which set him wandering here and there, wherever shipwrecks might carry him, to know the world and human beings; his earthy and wise language, which made him understood by all, as though he spoke in several tongues; but above all his body's misshapen, potent, simian, hunchbacked and theatrical ugliness; in sum, the adventures of his life made Aesop the perfect paradigm for his own *Fables* and for ours, because this man, said to be the primal father of the fabulous, belongs to it rather, as model, vignette, illustration or, better still, the basic soil, as though the *Fables* related in detail the currency of his body. The *Life of Aesop*, that's the title of the founding apologue every fabulist must write; as if this canonical man's body and language imitated the bodies and language of animals, plants, mountains, kings and cobblers. The fables' corpus relates Aesop's body in detail.

How is Aesop's body able to project itself so easily into every species? Victor Hugo gave one of his main characters, who resembled the fabulist, a nickname which summarizes my words, Quasimodo, a name that means "as if": like animals, like other men and things, by taking their place, by substituting oneself for them, by acting like them, by portraying them and simulating them. Deformed, the bell ringer's body appears monstrous because it can take on a thousand forms. These mimetic gymnastics explain fables, stories and theater, totems and fetishes, but dive, deeper still, into the acquisition of knowledge. They no doubt even transcend cultural barriers, like a common corpus. No doubt universal, at least fundamental, in every way transcendental, this body shows the sum of our bodies and also the well that archaic knowledge comes out of, brought up from the bottom of the ages by fables. As ugly, in sum, as Aesop and Quasimodo, lastly we have Socrates, a scholar without writing, reciting fables before dying and whose wisdom Plato deciphers on the teaching body.

RETURN TO COPYING: THE WEAKNESS
AND FRAGILITY OF ABSTRACTION

Whence the same wisdom, perhaps which comes over Rousseau, Bouvard and Pécuchet when they decide, toward the end of life, to copy out books and music. They ground themselves in the global conduct of the things of the world, of the depths of life and the body's wrinkles. Quasimodo: they make like the flesh and grass, like the wildflower, which replicate the characteristics of their family; re-producing for the sake of reproducing; knowing therefore for the sake of loving. Are they abandoning ideas?

Unique and sown with leafy circumstances, neither the species nor the individual, neither the fact, nor the landscape, neither this protein, nor any given star, in a word the singular, can be understood by means of general ideas. All we can do is describe, draw, copy them out, reproduce, represent, in short, imitate them point by point and detail after detail. Knowledge of this singularity begins with the art of copying. The sum of copies, the memory, then, is justly regarded as being the only knowledge. Memories, in their turn, objects, inert or technological, living bodies, the world, lastly, know the way recording media or subjects do.

God doubtless does not have general ideas, since He knows the least of His creatures and since there isn't a single hair on my head He hasn't counted. He relates to individuals in their details; His memory encompasses every one of them. Humans conceive general ideas because, deficient, their memory is in no way sufficient to embrace everything. Abandoning circumstances, planing down the details, they invent laws which enable them to deduce and foresee, that is, with an insufficient memory, to imitate God. An economy of thought, abstraction compensates for this deficiency. Invent a powerful enough memory, and there will be no more need to economize: behold computers. Because they accumulate singular landscapes within, because they store the details of individuals in memory, they have the right to take their denomination from medieval theology: *Deus ordinator omnium*. They resemble my body.

Second Stage:
Body to Body with Things

Imitation leads a person to face another; but simulation chains a person to a thing. Primitive, collective practices precede objective experience: cause before the thing. Ball, puck, button... the quasi-object precedes and constructs the object because it marks out the relations between the players; money, a general equivalent, replaces all relations. We mimic one another, we oppose one another; suddenly, one of us leaves the cage of causes and, outside this mimetic prison, discovers all alone, a thing – behold invention.

His body assimilates it. Returned, afterwards, amidst the causes, this thing, wholly new, becomes again the cause of new oppositions....

For, while learning requires the corporal imitation of others, it quickly falls into habit and, worse, into obedience. A teaching that places pupils and mediocre teachers face to face leads to slavery and prohibits the freedom to think for oneself. Peer pressure teaches, but the jealousy it entails produces imbeciles. Consequently, when invention suddenly appears, it throws itself, outside causes, into the imitation of things. Not toward the gestures of others, stiffened and become specific; not into the sound of their voices, but into the musical imitation of the sounds of the blacksmith at work, without being concerned about just who is striking the anvil, as it is said Pythagoras did, at the origin of arithmetic; not into the imitation of the power of pharaohs, but into the shadow of their tombs, and without regard for their absolute power, like Thales at the origin of geometry; not into the rival tyrants' race for power and without regard for their gold crowns, but into the bathtub where Archimedes gauges their density, in order to judge whether they be counterfeit or genuine; not into the imitation of those who light the fire, but into the burning pit of the flames themselves, like Empedocles throwing himself headlong into one of his theory's elements, at the bottom of one of Etna's craters. *Adæquatio rei et intellectus* begins with *adæquatio rei et corporis*. Jacques Monod used to tell me he had lower back pain to such a degree his back was twisted into a DNA helix. What is this *adæquatio*, except a *mimêsis* otherwise and better fitted?

Everyone can measure, on these typical bodies, the distance between learning and invention. Hence the impression a good many human sciences give us nowadays: we always already know what they claim to teach us, since they do nothing but continually make explicit the whole of the imitations in which our body has been immersed, ever since we began, for better or for worse, to live together, in the midst of other bodies, without which we would never have become men participating in our culture and language. Hence the converse impression of novelty the hard sciences give us: we never know in advance just what they are going to teach us, since they are always shifting away from the imitation of others toward the simulation of the world: always surprising and hidden, things differ from men, always political or repetitive, archaic and originary. And so, at the end of our route, here lies the end of imitation, in both senses of the word *end*: burial and intention, death and resurrection.

GEOMETRY AND PROPORTIONS

Diogenes Laertius, *Lives, Doctrines, and the Sayings of Famous Philosophers* (Thales, I, 27): "Hieronymus says that Thales measured the pyramids by their shadows, taking the observation at the time of day when our own shadow is equal to our height." Thus homothety was born, equivalent of mimetism when turned toward things. Never have we come so near the origins, since among the primitive theorems, Thales' theorem on the similarity of triangles is considered the first one conceived. But neither has the body imitated so well the things of the Earth – those rocks under which, once again, lies a dead body – while at the same time imitating the things of the Sky, since the hour when the shadows are equal is read on a sundial. The enormous pile of rocks and the body standing upright, both taken as *gnomon*, block at the same time and in the same way the light of the Sun. Let's call homothety this harmony of the shadows of the Earth beneath the clarity of the Sky. Not only does this story bring to the fore the body's role in the invention of the theorem, but it also stages the passage from the imitation of bodies to the reproduction of objects by them or even of objects among themselves, without further consideration of the subjects themselves: for, at Giza, the three pyramids reproduce among themselves, already similar by a Thales' theorem that precedes the geometer. But why position himself here rather than under the Lighthouse of Alexandria or the Colossus of Rhodes? Because it's a question of hatred for Kheops, something with which Herodotus's pages overflow, because it's a question of death. Under Ra's blinding light, Thales' body or that of another, standing, prevails over the Pharaoh's body, forever lying under the colossal lapidation. Intelligent, the weak has just killed the strongest. And the new imitation rejoins the conflict.

Now, to signify the end of these conflicts in the justice of equitable balance sheets, one of the first simple machines, the balance, equipped with "arms" and symmetry (another name, wholly objective, for imitation), seems an almost human form: a skeleton that measures peace by the stable cessation, perfect on both sides, of all inegalitarian iniquity. The two pans can, nevertheless, support different weights; to return to a level beam, the length of the arms only needs to be changed. As with a harmonious organism, a relationship is established, then, between that variable reach and the different masses; the same, or symmetrical imitation, is re-established by the compensated inequalities of the arms and weights. Now, after whole numbers, the first mathematical formalization utilized proportions and analogies (another and yet another name for mimetism): this is to that as something else is to a fourth. Comparing a comparison, relating two relations amounts to expanding mimetism from strict equality to a broader relation and from two terms to a longer series. Applied to the two arms, equal or unequal, this first analogy of proportions equally opens up mechanics, from which follow not only the physical sciences and technologies, but also the laws of exchange, for economics, and a model of justice. A primitive form, the balance thus recruits several primitivities: the cessation of struggles, first, then the beginnings of algebra, of mechanics and physics, of economics and morality, of straight justice and knowledge's exact precision; that's our body where the left imitates the right. With regard to the beginnings of fluid mechanics, we shall see, at vertigo's end, Archimedes in ecstasy.

ASTRONOMY

The sky is sown with the limbs of women, men and animals: Betelgeuse, the shoulder; Rigel, the foot; the Virgin; Hercules, the athlete; Orion, the hunter... Lion, Scorpion, Capricorn... as though the parts and gestures of the body expanded out to the stars: the sky and the body inter-imitate. Ovid recounted how some deadly tragedies had crucified those pieces of flesh on the constellations, by mimicking their form and arrangement. And if these bloody *Metamorphoses* taught us the true paths of knowledge, from the body to the species – stag and wolf, swallow and spider, oak

and linden – to things and stars, via imitations and
rivalries, love and hate, doubles and transformations...
my entire thesis, better painted in unbearable images?
And if empiricism's work appeared more concretely
in Ovid than in Locke and Condillac? And were
Donkey Skin told to me, I should see in it an extreme
philosophy.... After having recommended *The Art of
Loving*, by the body, did the Latin poet know that he
wrote the Art of Knowing, by the same body? Did
he, like all fabulists, draw his inspiration from myths
dating back to eras without writing?

TRANSCENDENTAL FLEXIBILITY

Does a fundamental suppleness condition this
metamorphic power, as did, a little while ago, the
whiteness deciphered in sleep, old age and the
Transfiguration? Stiff and hard, neither the tree, nor
even the reptile possesses this fundamental flexibility:
who has seen a donkey capable of reverence? Because
this flexibility allows us to pass from the hard to the
soft, it inaugurates and conditions knowledge. A
foundry, it permits us to flow into any form. Air or
water, low basic viscosity, prime matter, it can be split
up without being divided, like tongues of fire; certain
glottises, tongues, legs, heads..., having become
marvelously supple, enable singing, pleading cases,
dancing or feigning emotions; but sometimes this
fluidity inundates, infuses, aerates, little by little,

the totality of the body whose performance then rises, with its level, toward globality, thus, it seems to me, toward more intelligence and comprehension, as though every organ had to go into a trance, through this basic flexibility, to attain invention. The body angels have gives a quite faithful image – white and transparent, appearing and disappearing – of this incandescent fire, but the best one, assuredly, remains the image of the breath of the soul, the breath of that aerial spirit whose lucidity befalls a body whose entirety attains the utmost of flexibility, or fills with its liquid to the volatile limit. Not only does knowledge come out of the body's metamorphoses, but the soul or spirit both express this white volatility: should we give this new meaning to the expression: esprit de corps? Do animals lack a soul, so as to belong to singular species that are so rigid that said animals cannot free themselves from their rigor? Either the species or the soul: membership or intelligence, there is no middle ground: so choose your metamorphosis, either mobile or fixed, either the pliant process or one of its avatars; so decide, then, on your camp, your party, your corporation, your opinion, and you will find yourself an ass, in the strict sense.

Little by little, through aging, death solidifies, since the spinal column and the joints of the limbs no longer afford as many degrees of freedom in stiffening, so that the soul flows out of the stiffened body, quitting and leaving behind a fixed and definitive grimace. Isn't it better to say the converse? That death consists in the exit of that little intelligence, supple and white, life, from a frozen rigidity?

First White Products

If the mind is born of the body's transparency, of its faculty or possibility of doing, the very first ideas must emerge from this virtuality, displaying these same characteristics. Here is the list, easy to draw up, of first white ideas: in logic, the tautology of identity; the empty subset in set theory; in arithmetic, the number zero; early geometry's homogeneous, smooth, isotropic and transparent space, heralded, long ago, by Anaximander's indefinite; the x, the algebraic unknown, which can, because it has none in particular, take on any value; equation, equivalence; static equilibrium, uniform motion, the dynamic or thermodynamic constancy of forces; matter; the tautological idea of life... here are the foundations, transparent and white, of the principal sciences... and if the so-called social sciences cannot arrive at genuine knowledge, this is due, in large part, to the fact that not one of them has managed to form a single basic idea of this kind, ideas whose origins are found in that empty, smooth and translucent white box, the body's indefinite capacity to transform. This leads to the paradox: how does it happen that the

94

most objective and hard sciences approach nearer the body and better than those sciences which, it might be expected, should speak of it the most closely.

A Noisy, Sonorous, Vocal, Musical, Reasonable Interlude

All that has preceded was done and said in the total absence of sound. Is there a secret concealed in the imitation of noise and music, one so tenuous that it accounts for the passage between procedural information – still bound to the figures and processual cross-fading of movements – and symbolic information, more arbitrary: the very transition between gesture and speech? This is what differentiates the deaf from the blind and explains why the latter can enter into the abstract more easily than the former, attached in a harder way to the procedural information of the hands and body. As supplely as the body may point or sign, it can't equal the spell of the volatile and voluble plastic art of voices. What could be more natural than that music precedes, accompanies, follows, haunts dance? Then it passes on to the phonogram, to the mixture of respirations, hoarse cries of desire, groans of pain, then to the duet, trio, quartet and choir, toward reasonable dialogue... pas de deux, court of love, amœbean verse, conversation....

The teaching body dances its knowledge softly so that the audience will, like it, go into a trance and so that, through virtual mimicry of its gestures, a few ideas will enter their heads via the muscles and bones, which though seated and immobile are solicited, pulled toward the beginnings of movement, perhaps even by the written work's little jig. The auditors adopt the same imaginary postures sleepers do when dreaming; fascinated, the body imitates the form indicated by the dancer-model and his narrative or imagines itself imitating it: behold, already, an installed schema. It's known that the neurons that control an actual gesture and those that do so for a gesture which is seen and, thus, mimicked solely in virtuality, both discharge the same amount of electricity. Number and letter, addition or language, all things that are difficult to realize for the position-adopting body, this is the teacher's ballet, real, which the receptors reproduce, in potentiality only. No doubt ballerinas and clowns, tragic or comedic, orators, pulpit or political, in the church or at the circus, teach, likewise, rites, postures and sentiments, to their gaping spectators, but the instructor body must, in addition, present itself without affectation or cosmetic, without décor or adornment, in order to make them believe that it isn't dancing or performing, so much do the sciences, hard, reject every flourish, so that it has to perform them in a puritanical lecture hall that condemns all performance. For, should its arm and voice utilize the full range of their grandiloquence, they lose all plausibility; but, conversely, should they refrain from all effect, learning, immediately, misses its mark.

A soft trance, what does this mean? Two things, one of which is hard. In its origin, violent, *transir* meant, in fact, to go into death pangs: a sculpture of a cadaver was called a transi. A trance reproduces the dance that seizes an organism when in the throes of its final moments, a dance whose movements, desperate, seek to escape the terminal violence of the inevitable Reaper. An invisible adversary attempts to clinch it in holds it evades: the whole combination of these escapes, retreats, breaks, evasions, evokes the defenses displayed in fencing or boxing. Is it only the struggle, invisible and forgotten, with death which captivates in dance and eloquence? Is it only the risks incurred by the clown or the lion tamer, the tragedian and the dancer, that make them worthy of admiration? What danger must the teaching body risk in order to attract attention? Humble, it dives into knowledge that infinitely exceeds it, and embarked on this sea at the risk of shipwreck, it grapples with error, noise and gibberish... a young Jacob, valiant little soldier, passing the night wrestling with the Angel, more learned than he, the spirit of death, before whom, since his partner, spiritual, does not appear, those present think they see him dancing.

A soft trance, hence through language. Should a tiny demon take shelter in the cavern of the mouth, what gymnastics it would behold: the glottis and the tongue against the gums, lips and palate, what a ballet! Just as the written work dances the jig, by means of the fingers and strokes' braids and loops, speech executes a thousand and one physical contortions. *Soft*, here, means that the trance descends an entire scale of size and power, from the body to one of its small organs, as though, from the concrete to the abstract, the passage required an intermediary reduced-scale model. The miniaturization of the body's actions and positions is lodged between the thing and its logical or formal schema. The Italians and French gesticulate while speaking so as to unfold the complete spectrum of semaphore: from the large dance to the medium, from the ballerina to the tongue, and then toward the small dance, toward the true softness of meaning. Just as, thumping the boards of the platform, striking the tambourine or attached to castanets, the sardana is given rhythm and jerkings by the heels, wrists and phalanges, so the noisy and sonorous emission of the column of air expired by the thorax and larynx is broken, continued or modulated according to the figures, baffles and dams of this dance of the tongue. Vocalises, appeals, cries, confessions, spoken sentences... model, by miniaturizing them, the body's metamorphoses. Is it still a question of a dance to the death? What pressing danger does each sound evade? Our first body cried its first sorrow at the first loss of the beloved feminine body; thus the final body in its final loss mourns all the loves from which it proceeded. Speak then for several minutes before a crowd to learn how much these discreet but not mute gymnastics protect you from the virtual lynching promised by the cooperation of the pack whose silent eyes converge on your lips.

Do these corporal simulations and then these figurines of dance in the mouth descend next to the icons of writing, hieroglyphics that formerly imitated things and animals? Do these successive miniaturizations go as far as the ballets performed by the acids and proteins in the cell's organelles, as far as the combinations of atoms in crystals and molecules? What coded choreographies must be deciphered at each level of the size scale?

And since, beyond proprioceptive descriptions, I've come to objective biology, why not take note here of the association of the brain and the cerebellum, the latter governing gestures and the former thoughts? The cerebellum, in charge of postural reactions and the coordination of movement, fills the role of preliminary transmitter: as the transition between the body's postural reactions and the brain, does it open up the passage this genesis of knowledge requires?

IMITATION AND CONFLICT

That, like an original sin, violence – imitation's companion from learning's origin – remains one of knowledge's latest and best achievements should not, as children of Hiroshima, Seveso and the attempts at eugenics, surprise us. The violence of knowledge is less the result, as was believed, of its relations to power than the result of its very birth; violence remains attached to it like the tail to its comet. The explosion over Nagasaki, which in August, 1945, ended the confrontation between the West and the Far East, must be deciphered as a trace of Abel's murder, at the end of his rivalry with Cain: how does one learn, and what, without mimicking one's brother, and so closely that one ends up by taking his place? The victor in a war sometimes becomes the twin of the vanquished: the blow for blow rendered them identical. Nothing is free, everything has its price, including progress, invention and discovery. Why should knowledge escape from this iron law that nothing comes from nothing? Just as imitation becomes generalized at the knowing's birth, likewise conflict becomes amplified on the side of knowledge. Global divas, the nuclear physicists responsible for the Manhattan Project in the Nevada desert slandered and tore at one another n as many battles for glory as any number of mobsters from rival pressure groups; their antagonism carried on so much so that, despite the deaths of the two Japanese ports, they didn't think twice about pushing their research all the way to bombs thousands of times deadlier. Competition, another name for mimicry, exposes us to every danger, including in the sciences.

By mimicking others, we love them and hate them; but, in addition, ever since the Greek dawn, we have also imitated things, and the same conclusions must be drawn from this: we serve them and destroy them. The same ethics, therefore, applies to things as to men: as well as the latter, our knowledge must preserve the world, and serve, as well, toward the end of the conflict that opposes us to this world. Hence, a law and a morality, equivalent, both given expression in *The Natural Contract*.

THREE BEGINNINGS

During the years, known as miraculous, of sixth century Greece, the abstract geometry of similarities was therefore born from the concrete body that imitates, at the same time as astronomy, mechanics and, I haven't said it, the geography of the Earth, since the measurement of the latitudes was derived from the sundial. Now, during the Renaissance, in the same year or almost, 1543, three maps came to be: a map of the sky, modeled by Copernicus; another terrestrial globe, projected by the geographer Mercator; and a new body, drawn on Vesalius's anatomical plates. Lastly, this very day, we are introducing three pages of the body, earth and sky to the modern era: a Universe whose photons reach us from billions of years in time and millions of light-years in space; an Earth that has been explored, to the very centimeter from satellite height, down to its innermost movements: we watch volcanoes breathe and maritime abysses slowly open; finally or firstly, we are detailing the body's biochemical and genetic constitution.

These three landscapes carry us toward the future. In these three moments which we can regard as beginnings begun again, the presence of the human body harmonically summarizes my arguments.

A Computer Science Model of the Thesis

By way of conclusion, I now put forward the hypothesis that the body's metamorphoses and learning's mimetism function as software; gestures bear the same relationship to anatomical assemblies and physiological and biochemical functions as, in a machine, software does to hardware.

We don't confuse the vertical hoisting crane and the cement mixer which, in turning, mixes its load. We can tell the difference between a monkey wrench and a socket wrench due to their form and function, linked to each other. A tool, a simple machine, a motor, an automaton first present a topography, parts arranged in space in a certain manner for a certain use. For these parts and this assemblage, in addition, to function, they receive or produce force: the muscular arm on the winch crank, the draft horse, steam, electricity, liquid or nuclear fuel. Fixed, their topography renders their response to every external impulse constant, just as with animals. Descartes was right to describe animals as machines, provided the latter be limited to the couple topology-energetics and the former to the doublet anatomy-physiology, form and force which determine the instinct or usage reaction. Here, the model imitates the organism.

Information, Software and Program

But a common novelty is attained for computers, those new machines, and the body by introducing an intermediary between form-force and function. As infinitesimal energy bound to the arrangement of things and signs, information plays the role, at least vaguely, of this new intermediary agency. For a computer, moreover, software is the name given to the set of information suitable for programming the machine, that is, to change its behavior, while the material arrangement of its parts doesn't change, thus transforming the old machine into a new one; said machine can then be called universal. Software transforms the hardware, just as the body is transformed by its gestures and mimickings in this book. So the sought after intermediary consists of information, software and program. The union of the soul to the body or the understanding to the somatic is as clear and difficult as the relation of software to hardware.

Hardware Information, Software Information

Returning first to the spatial arrangement of the machine, let's term hardware the information that cannot vary without changing this form; tied to the anatomy, fixed, instinct, in the living being, fits this definition. If, on the other hand, information can vary without any change in this anatomy, it is to be called software. Corporal imitation allows the spatial position of the limbs to vary without any change in their arrangement, so as to add a quantity of software information – all the larger because training enables this repertory of gestures to multiply or diversify – to the elementary hardware information.

Software entails the set of information that governs the machine's conduct and enables, through its own modifications, this conduct to be modified at will; imitation carries the information that governs and modifies the body's conduct in the same way. Software makes the machine programmable or makes its behavior first and foremost transformable from the outside. Imitation makes the body adaptable and indefinitely flexible.

Now neither the respective material arrangement of the body's organs nor their anatomy, nor the physiology of its organic systems is ever altered by the body's diverse positions; the body's material information therefore does not change. Before taking up these positions or after having left them behind, the body can be said to be pre-posed or reposed... yes, invariant through the most exacting variations of flexibility and valor, of mimicry and courage.

Now – let there be no mistake – the variable gestural repertory of this gymnast, actor or dancing body transmits considerable information without, I'll say it again, altering the body's anatomy or its physiology: therefore the body is overflowing with software information which, in turn, is divided into procedural and symbolic information according to whether imitation retraces the thing itself – the foot or its trace for the walker's step – or installs an arbitrary relation between the thing and itself, the number one, for example, and this raised finger.

INNATE IDEAS

Now the computer differs from every other machine in that it records programs which thus pass from the exterior into its memory. Consequently, no one can truly distinguish anymore between program and data. Likewise, the human body differs from instinctual animal anatomies in that it is capable of recording an enormous sum of gestural sequences as integrated corporal schemata. Consequently, no one can truly distinguish between external imitation and personal habits. In both cases, this aptitude permits the creation of programs that modify themselves or produce others. Truly historical, such a process makes the computer attain the dignity of a universal machine and the human body the possibility of universal knowledge, which is what I wanted to demonstrate.

Who, then, will distinguish between external data, termed sensible, and the traces termed internal of old deposited programs? One can perceive the vanity of the quarrel between the sensualists – partisans of external impressions – and the nativists – partisans of always already deposited ideas – over the question of the origin of knowledge, since, precisely, universality, for us as for these machine-models, only arises from this continual process of supple integration of mimetically learned and reproduced schemata.

Falsification of the Origin

No, one will say, imitation can't preside over the origin of knowledge, since it mimics someone who would already be in possession of it. How, then, did this latter acquire it? By imitating. But, dash it, by imitating whom? Another person for whom the same question is posed once again: and so on ad infinitum. Now we see the same thing with machines. Ever since we began manufacturing and using computers, we have had at our disposal software that have transformed these machines so that an already quite long history has made them such as we see them today. Should an improbable event destroy all programs and software, we couldn't just resume that history at the very point of and starting from that destruction. We would have to begin everything all over again from scratch. We have already forgotten the entire learning process.

The same holds true for knowledge: we've lost all that took place during the mimetic processes flowing since the dawn of time. Should an improbable event deprive us tomorrow of language, for example, we should have to begin everything all over again from scratch, and the recovery of linguistic expertise would cost us a length of history equivalent to the one disappearing in the shadows behind. Thus, this long history improves imitation slowly: the passage to infinity is only valid for logical reasoning and not this patient adaptation which saw, sometimes, the mimicker improve the mimicked in his gesture, and made the body an ensemble of memories so well-engrammed that certain philosophers even believed – and believe still – in the innate origin of knowledge and language. Incapable of evaluating the patient labor of time, we forget the metamorphic work of memorization.

MEDITATION, MEDICATION

If knowledge begins with imitation, the former, in return, rebounds back onto the body, making it supple and rejuvenating it from joining in a *pas de deux* with intelligence. Honest and intense, every meditation generates a medication: thought bestows health, research brings about a salutary joy, and beauty halos invention – generous and soothing – with its radiance, just as the absence of idea can render ugly, coarse, jealous, sickly and old.

The balanced diet of early infancy, the quality of life and hygiene, the less exhausting physical labor, the pharmacology and medicine – above all the preventative kind – have all recently produced a new senior citizen, a more youthful one than in any preceding generation. Let's mention three ways to stay young: first, the aforementioned cosmetics, dying the hair or so-called aesthetic surgery.... But breasts soon sag once more and wrinkles deepen again, jet black hair goes back to being yellowish while the dewlap sways back and forth with every motion. Stupid old hag or ridiculous old fart trying to act young, nobody escapes the body's falling. Spread by advertising, this method, expensive, remains quite ineffective. The second way requires physical exercise and diet: early to bed, rising likewise, giving up sugars, fats, alcohol and tobacco, walking two hours a day, never stepping out from under the yoke. Lesser known, this way, inexpensive, and more effective, already requires a morality. Lastly, young or old, dotards suffer from cerebral softening. One can distinguish already, one will distinguish even better tomorrow the disabled drivelers, who every evening, for thirty years, have watched the made-for-TV movies exported by America in order to ensure the mental and physical debility of the world, from the quick and vigorous intelligences who spend their evenings reading difficult books; living in the excellence of thought, they laugh. The imbecile is measured by repetition and sadness, sprightly intelligence by joyful novelty. The most beautiful civilizations begin with laughter. Why hesitate to say it? Culture alone protects from the senility produced, on the contrary, by the absence of intellectual exercise. Effective and free, this final way of preserving youthful dynamism remains – oh, surprise – unknown. Friend Doctor, do you prescribe some difficult page seasoned with reasoning to your patients as a remedy for the pervading debility that threatens us all, you as well as me, with devastatingly sudden aging?

Plato's name means broad-shouldered; Corneille sweat in blankets of coarse wool before sitting down to write; Diderot and Rousseau walked every day, at first together, and later separately.... Chateaubriand climbed aloft by the ratlines between the shrouds faster than the master sailors could. You'll recognize thought without fail by the health it gives. The two of them converse together and with their sister immortality.

Vertigo

A summit ridge, sometimes, draws out into a long sharp knifeblade, whose tapering keenness looks out over the vertical walls on which some of the gods of alpinism win renown in every season of the year. I often have difficulty standing on this high knife's edge, so vertiginous does this vertical circle appear. Although it's possible to suffer the agonies of true vertigo in one's bed, at ground level, what's invoked under this name so as to excuse oneself for not climbing mountains amounts to nothing but panic. An equilibrial disorder as frequent in the plains as it is in elevated positions, vertigo, pathological and rare, is distinct from acrophobia, the cowardly and normal anxiety of a perched body.

The Upright Posture:
Vertical on Vertebrae

Constructed like the adjective *vertical*, which describes both cliffs and our stature, the word *vertigo* is similar, as well, to the vertebrae of the column that bears our body. For these three terms repeat the preposition *vers* [towards], their root, whose double meaning is surprising; translation in a direction: I'm going towards Paris..., but also, and almost conversely, rotation, since *vers* originates in the Latin *verto*, signifying turning, possible gyration thanks to our vertebrae. How can the same word indicate, at one and the same time: going in a straight line and turning? Might the skeleton resemble that rigid staff surrounded by serpentine volutes, as though in a helix, that was called Hermes' caduceus? Or the form of a strand of DNA, to which everyone owes their traits? How does it happen, likewise, that we say, heedlessly, that things are taking a turn, when, precisely, they're going in a direction that's in actual fact determinate? What strange relation does our upright and vertical posture maintain with the turns of these vertebrae? Do we experience the spins, standing?

We can't learn this, alas, by asking children – without language during the days of their first steps – about their impressions, nor remember the inaugural moment when an anthropoid ancestor went from four hands to two feet. Did he stagger along, for his entire life, with the trouble children display for only a few weeks? Why does the effort to hoist ourselves toward the vertical circle throw us to the ground, caught in a vortex? Because this ascent opens, little by little, the angle of the back, closed when, leaning over, we walked on four hands? How did we unbend ourselves?

THE HUNDRED METERS

A former amateur in the eight hundred and thousand meters, I admire what I have never succeeded in practicing, speed. The adaptation to the brief bursting forth at the sound of the gun haunts me; I never saw anything but the backs of my concurrents, well-named for once. By the way, how long does this hundred meters last? Ten seconds, you reply, in the best of cases; thirteen to fourteen otherwise; after that no one keeps track. No, four million years. You jest!

Not in the least. And first, what reason, natural or otherwise, is there for requiring the athletes to place themselves, at the start, crouched, as though on all fours, the back quasi-horizontal, the front limbs propped on the track's surface, one knee on the ground and the other bent in front? Because they launch out better that way, you reply. Assuredly, but look then at the body's semi-bent position in the first moments of the race: we all began this way, of course not the brief Olympic race toward medals of imitation gold, but rather the race clocked by another timepiece, the one whose duration leads us from a quadrumanous position to the upright posture – definitively or temporarily human – that the runners adopt, stopped, on the podium, proud; our ancestors would not have been able to stand there, erect and immobile. We thus stood up extremely slowly and through the same successive profiles that the runners display during that ten second flash of lightning. Film them then and project their images as slowly as possible: stupefaction, pure paleoanthropology unfolds.

Scarcely descended from the trees, our ancestors enjoyed in fact, at the start, a double locomotion, quadrumanous and bipedal: during this interminable interval of doubt, in which the joints of the arm show themselves to be, as with Lucy's remains, for example, as powerful as the floating ones of the knee, did they walk? Nothing could be less certain. Our precursors trundled along instead, rolling like a small boat, exactly the way our athletes rise at the initial sound of the gun, and begin running in a semi-bowed position, one doubly characteristic of our mad sprints and anthropoid apes, still a little crouched, the back and the head stooped forward, not entirely unfolded, the animated movements of the anterior and posterior limbs not yet aligned along the axis of the course.

'm not dreaming: in his thesis, *Le Syndrôme de Lucy chez les footballeurs* [The Lucy Syndrome in Soccer Players] (Medical thesis, University of Paris-VII, 1992), Dr. Sylvain Dionnet, a specialist in sports medicine, shows that more than half the injured soccer players he examined suffered from muscle strain in the ischiotibial muscles, shortened, precisely, by the body's initial straightening up, therefore not adapted because of this too brief and rapid running. So take off as fast as possible, and you'll necessarily return to the anthropopithecine profile, abandoned little by little, thus to the progressive unbending we admire in the proposed film. Everyone, the winner and losers, arrives upright.

From the starting blocks to the podium, by passing through the energetic start, the acceleration, the unfolding and finish line of these hundred meters, our champions of speed spark enthusiasm in us because they make us relive in abridged form the corporal memory, complete and immemorial, of our hominization: millions of years of evolution in a lightning curve of ten seconds. Look at the winner, proud on the podium: the hominin standing upright, like everyone.

But, it occurs to me, we can, also, remember such originary states, whether childish or age-old, when we learn, later on, to stay up on and ride a bicycle. What a very strange instrument, one that stands, all the stabler, and goes, all the straighter, it too, when it turns. Those who believe that the upright posture founds its stable position on two foot arches, wide enough to form, with the interval between the legs, the famous support polygon, and who view us as though we were a statue on its socle – this last word signifying, precisely, the sabot – do they understand this triple defiance of balance on a narrowband tire, above a circle, in addition, and in motion, to top it off? And yet we'll soon seat ourselves comfortably on this saddle that overhangs these casters!

Walk, run or dance, now, and note that the multiple and flexibly articulated movements of the thighs, calves, knees and ankles propagate, underneath the foot, starting from the heel, perhaps continuously, up to the metatarsal head and the toes, as though the entire arch of the foot were unfolding, round or convex, and not as an interior and concave vault. If our legs, motionless, rest, sometimes, completely stiff, on the points of stilts, they roll, on the march, on elastic tire segments, continually repeated, starting from the attack of the calcaneus and breaking off at the tips of the toes. We move, the way a porch swing, cradle, rocking horse or chair oscillates in place. We stand on two flat bases, no doubt, but we move about on two small segments of circumference, for, contrary to the curve of their arches, the feet function as arcs. Where do the so intense delights brought by walking and running come from? From the fact that each step, each stride rolls without jumping, elastic and continuous, passing through the hollow of the sole to raise itself toward the tips of the toes: the foot, a flight board, changes these two promenades into promises of ecstasy.

Furthermore, since we don't always walk or run on level surfaces, the pitch or the slope of mountains, the oblique furrows, the inclines cut across with irregular paving stones bring circles into play perpendicular to the one just mentioned, at the risk, sometimes, of twisting an ankle. Starting at the foot, we find ourselves mounted on gimbals, on two wheels or four, not counting the curves of the path on which we change direction. The legs, as for them, form the spokes of several other spheres, with the knee and the hip as axles or hubs: make like a compass and walk, as the rich like to say. We find ourselves, already, on bicycles, better on *birouettes* as the *brouette* [wheelbarrow] was called during the Grand Century, when it still ran on two wheels. How many of them must we count? The lower body is plunged into bundles or, better, networks of spheres: it glides on a thousand ball bearings. The rotations expressed by the terms *vertigo* and *vertebra*, but curiously forgotten in the adjective *vertical*, are found then, demultiplied, in the lower limbs and beneath the soles of the feet. We think ourselves straight and stiff, kingly bearing, queenly carriage.... But no! We pitch and roll, little boats floating without submersion, on rough seas.

However difficult to develop for the industrial and metallic reasons of minimal friction, to make its appearance, at least in its principle, the bicycle only required the knowledge of running or walking: a great many wheels already existed there.

CASTING OFF: INVENTION

We therefore did not, to my knowledge, have to invent the wheel, since we had carried many, from time immemorial, beneath us. Their corporal presence exempted us from even having to discover it. But how, without invention or discovery, did it come to be? Through a process of casting off, of setting sail.

In the sense of a punctured basket or cask, the body leaks. Our organs sometimes empty themselves of their forms and functions, so as to pour them outside. Yes, our limbs cast off, which means that they leave us so as to form apparatus, tools similar to them, but cast off from them. Thus the hands unmoored the hollows of their palms: spoon or shovel; their fingers:

fork and pitchfork; their index fingers and opposable thumbs: chopsticks or combination pliers... and so many other implements so as to devote themselves, afterward, to other exercises, which they will, later on, concretize into other fashioned objects; likewise, the arms leave, outside, levers or weapons... and the limbs in general, their gestures and movements deposit tools or machines into the exterior; thus, the memory often empties itself of its stores onto pages, books and libraries; the imagination abandons its icons onto paper, canvas or screen; the intelligence hands its operations over onto the sundial or the calculator....

Yes, our body rids and lightens itself; and how, indeed, could it undertake new adventures, did it not set down, along the evolutionary roadsides, the various loads of what it knows how to do, already? Other inventions will follow from the virginity rediscovered at the times of these castings off. As soon as writing unloaded our memories onto parchments, we discovered abstract geometry; as soon as printing freed us from the necessity of remembering, we invented physical experiments. These externalized apparatus produce, in sum, a history I call exo-Darwinian evolution, as though Darwinism itself came little by little from us, as though evolution percolated among these objects. As for it, the animal remains that enclosed fortress, the walls of stupidity which prevent it from ridding itself of its acquired or instinctive assemblies, which therefore compel it to repeat them, whereas man, divested of this curtain wall, the naked animal, porous, leaks and pours its capacity into space: what I call casting off. Here then are our scattered limbs dispersed throughout nature, technological objects, thus born. The tool doesn't extend the organ, it objectivizes it.

So the lower body lays its own wheelworks like eggs, and we find these rings again in carts, wheelbarrows and bicycles... bearing witness to our pedestrian circles; later, automobile tires and airplane landing gear will set the traces of our steps on the landscape going again in different motions. Our bodies are explained by machines, because they have already produced them.

For learning reverses this casting off. It suffices to find again, in the lower body, those wheels it has thrown into the world, those wheels whose fortune has increased so much and whose evolution has developed so much outside of it that the body no longer recognizes them as its own. Learning to ride a bicycle consists in feeling these wheels, integrated into the bike, through the rim and pedal, and feeling, by this very act, that we had never walked nor run except by their means, for we had invented upright posture, erect bearing and cadence, arising from the legs' circular torments, long before encountering them in objects, balanced through motion. Thus our every act of learning, slow, climbs back up the path of our inventions: come out of our bodies through strokes of genius, inventions return there in the family and at school.

THE MYSTERY OF THE TRANSUBSTANTIATION

Depending on age and circumstances, we learn to walk, run, the tennis serve, the carriage of the upper body, facial expressions, the courtly tact of love.... Mimicry, training, in short education and experience integrate new gestural sequences into our flesh: the body makes them so much its own it sometimes forgets them so as to better reproduce their schemata or vary on them, inventively. To give expression to this impression, we hesitate not at all to use digestive images such as assimilating: we incorporate what we learn. Drinking, eating, breathing, those necessary, conscious and deliberate acts make the inert, in fact, penetrate the organism's living unconsciousness: in proportion to digestion, it manufactures subject from certain objects. Since we don't have any transitive verb to express this process that is as quotidian as it is vital, and which concerns the body, in learning as well as in alimentation, I would prefer to say, beyond images, that it "subjectivizes" the things and movements it notices outside, thus rendering the objective subjective. How then are certain objects *subjectivized*? At the

121

refreshment stand, by manducation and inspiration imitation and learning.... Air, energy's fire, solid earth and waters are thus transubstantiated into my flesh and blood, but also the gestures and postures around me, but above all your body, to which mine returns like graces, caresses and pleasures.

The learned in physiology, thermodynamics or biochemistry teach us that the organism exchanges energy and information with its environment so as to conserve a certain invariance across the variations of life – squandering motions, growth and old age, the valiant struggle against disorder and the forces of death. Nothing could be more true, nothing so profound: we perpetuate our turbulences in deviation from lethal balance, while eating and drinking, a little, listening and breathing, a lot, loving essentially. But we don't just exchange energy to survive or information to smile.

When we receive things, we make them our own; we subjectivize them, in the sense just given the verb. Thus, toward the end of life, the body becomes entirely its own. I no longer remember a time when my flesh, virginal, was ignorant of every object, and yet my old body scarcely weighs on me under the null load of their enormous number; I only truly teach body to body, since most of my knowledge remains unconscious in the black box of this flesh, white from playing at virginity. Have I spent my life subjectivizing? Not at all, quite the contrary, I have exchanged, with all due respect, and not only ardent energy and this flow of rare chatter named information. Like many, I've produced objects, as such, yes, things: houses, books, plans carried out... limbs scattered everywhere of my objectivized body.

If we receive or take, we must also give back, since we exchange. To the process of subjectivization, which includes eating and drinking as well as learning and breathing, corresponds, as though by a symmetry of equilibrium, the process of objectification by which we sow our body throughout the world: we produce, in fact. Amidst this manufacturing, almost always repetitive, known as working, it happens, in rare moments, that a work invents. Then, a body lets fall outside itself – oh marvel! – one of its forms, one of its movements, a singular function, a hidden schema... in the form of a worldly object – a sledge-hammer, lever, mill, vessel or sonata, computer, theorem or poem; a fist becomes a hammer, an elbow an axle and fulcrum, a head a pocket calculator.... Then, this organ occurs like a big bang in the environment, supplied with a formidable quantity of hard or soft energy, an inexhaustible fount from which we drink... renewed at this strange wellspring by imitation and learning. Reducible to its corporal outline, a great invention spreads quickly in the world and multiplies in number because it sows the world like a seed. The Theban myth can be understood in this way, the one where in order to create the human race, the first woman sows, precisely, the scattered limbs of her mother by throwing them behind her, as though she knew how to do something she didn't understand.

Inventive production, so specifically human, counterbalances, counteracts, equilibrates, balances learning: the latter subjectivizes some object in the world, the first objectivizes all or part of the body. The body produces body, and the body produces world. It knows how to produce subjects, it can produce objects. Through assimilation, we create ourselves; we create newness, in return. Any education that merely teaches its flock to learn makes them into nothing but apes, not humans, those creative animals. The true life requires both arms of the balance: subjectivization and objectivization. We can give birth to things; we know, even within us, how to engender flesh.

Doubtless, I am not saying anything new here, since a divine word expressed this mystery before I did, better than I did. "This is my body; this is my blood," these two sentences signify that such worldly objects, bread or wine, are transubstantiated into Christ's flesh and blood; take this then and eat it each of you; take this and drink it each of you, this is what I named subjectivization; conversely, his flesh and blood are transubstantiated into this piece of bread and this goblet of wine, this is objectivization. Men in God's image, we transubstantiate objects into subjects as well as subjects into objects. Through the first action, life is maintained and develops, through the second one, culture comes into the world.

Virginity

Congested with behavioral schemata, animals remain stuck in a more than slow evolution of learning; jammed up with data, the congestion of their brains puts the brakes on their cognitive evolution, almost immobile. They resemble, like brothers, those imbeciles, often encountered in educated circles, who are sometimes besotted by their excess of knowledge. Knowledge increases with science, of course, but to the point of diminishing returns, where the more knowledge we have, the less we know. So we invented a way to counter this decrease: from time to time, we discharge this mass into things; we leak it; we empty our corporal schemata into castings off which become, thenceforth, savings of gestures, postures and movements, which become receptacles of objectivized behavior. The second moment of this unballasting consists in the equivalent purging of the brain, when we emptied our memory into writing, printing and computers. Evolution, then, continues on through them outside the body. After having given birth, this latter becomes virgin again and can, anew, produce the new: virgin and mother, without contradiction.

Ilinx: Seasickness and Seawellness

And the vertigo from which we started? Does it prevent us from learning or, on the contrary, does it accompany us, an ancient witness to our very first acts of straightening up? When we pass from the rounds of the legs and feet to those of wheels and pedals, do we experience the distress of the spins so as to get beyond it, after having severely experienced it, and in order to finally understand that the body undergoes it as an obstacle and makes use of it as a passage? Does it enjoy this vertigo or does it suffer from it?

Suffer from it, really? Why do you speak so often of its painful, yet quite rare distress? Have you forgotten then the delightful pleasures of the merry-go-round or the swing, on which the rear, instead of the foot, becomes integrated into the circular rotations that the vertebrae execute with ease? Roger Caillois called these rockers and tourneys Ilinx games, all diversions in which I always see and hear that same preposition *towards*. Did the nautical rollings of emotional lovemakings create, or, at least, precede, a thousand techniques and practices, musical or naval, also accompanied by intense enjoyment? You know, no doubt, as many women crazy for waltzing and other cadenced dances as men drunk with the sea, the women abandoned, like bacchantes, to rhythmic transports, by the flying gown and the soaring ecstasy, the men drunk with pitching, beaming with delight amid a few green faces vomiting forth their seasickness. Like those navigator's compasses that are all the more directionally stable when moved by all the more rapid rotations, do we owe our best balance to these whirlwinds or the vertical circle to these vortices?

Suffer from it, really? Let's remember, sailors, how much we fell faint during the bitter time needed to gain our sea legs before passing, one fine morning, into blissful health, soaring, ecstatic, like Hermes, the messenger god, on the two wheels, winged, of pitching and rolling combined, wheels strewn with unexpected eccentrics and cams. Restored to its best sense, vertigo contributes to the vertical circle, an even easier posture than in the past, as though the turbulent gentleness of the wind-driven rough seas deliciously oiled, greased, lubricated, anointed the hip, knee and ankle joints. Yes, rapid and unexpected rotations improve equilibrium; our language senses this when it speaks the vertical circle and its two senses. Who will sing the light-hearted levitation of this refined balance? Like those compasses kept constant by their gyroscopes, we find ourselves stabilized. We are continually repeating, while improving them, the primitive postures of the anthropoid and the child.

From Fluid Turbulences To Aerial Vortices

Stubbornly set, stupidly, on believing that we are wholly without elasticity on the earth, like ankylosed sticks on rigid crystals, we never think about fluid mechanics. But, the curve fluidifies the solid. Would we have become aware that we walk on the wheels of the legs and feet, had we not acutely experienced the marine turbine? Ah, I had forgotten to mention that in casting off we had just changed apparatus; though the navy prefers the word *tackle*. So in passing from walking to the bicycle, nothing, at bottom, changes, wheels for wheels, from the identical to the same, and again nothing changes when we embark and let ourselves go with the erotically circular movements of ships, except that our body becomes suppler and more fluid.

And even more so when it entrusts itself to an aircraft, at low altitudes, where the volatile turbulence temporarily puts in check, once more, and into an unsettling disorder, our semi-circular canals, the labyrinth of the inner ear and the vagal system. It's enough to have ridden out a "Gale from due north" in a small plane to learn how the world, one's body and that of one's female neighbor are perceived under these conditions. But I'll be damned, the organism knows how to go from simple rhythmic movements, step by step, toward periodic fluctuations whose complexity weds, for better or for worse, pitching and rolling, then energetically launches itself toward the chaotic oscillations of this fragile bird.

ORDER AND DISORDER: TOWARD LIFE

The organism can and wants to do it for, in its very construction, from the heart to the brain, it associates these vibrations. Set stupidly, at studying's end, on the laboratory table, the cardiac organ beats calmly, with a regular rhythm, whereas, living, right in the middle of the mediastinum, it integrates, allowing us to survive, the wanderings of chaos, suddenly as unpredictable as the noises that arise from the gray matter. Just as the regular clock neighbors the whimsical barometer on the partition in order to express in duet that the world is formed from order and disorder, likewise I love the cousinage, in my body, between the electrocardiogram, so stupid beneath its sine curves, and the electroencephalogram, chaotic with intelligent awakening. So where is the seat of emotion? I doubt that a tediously uniform heart would ever become flustered. Happily, science demonstrates that such regularity would put health in danger: we owe our health to nothing other than a chaotic heart.

Set out thus from equilibria of easy stability, like the quadrumanous and upright postures, at rest, toward fine stabilities discovered amidst more and more pitched about variations – round walking, listing bike, rolling vessel, turbulent plane... the lived adventure of this learning is equal to a fine voyage toward the center of life. Why? Countless are the shipwrecks of stable vessels, whereas the codfishermen of St. Pierre and Miquelon withstand the waves' fury, on their versatile dory, all the better when it rolls from side to side at the extreme risk of overturning, before the North Atlantic wind; the more it shifts, the less it founders, adapting itself to the high waves, the unexpected crashings of the surf, the dangerous breakers, all the more constant for its tossing, all the more sure for its pitching and rolling. Thus our body would go down with all hands should it enter that absence of agitation the sages of Antiquity called ataraxia; doubtless they never sailed. Menstruation, defloration, pregnancy and delivery, lactation and the return of menstruation... tempests all, lunar or chaotic, unknown to the masculine gender with its brief existence; this is one of the secrets of the longer lives of pouring and vertically-rotating women. How so?

Versatile and *overturning* give us the key to the secret. How, in fact, is the living body to be defined? Invariant, in a relative and temporary fashion, through weak deviations, then strong ones, at first round or periodic and then chaotic, dangers strengthen its stability, before destroying it, forever. Stable through variations, balanced through instabilities, organized through disorders, ordered through disruptions, invariant and versatile lastly, the living being goes toward: this is the stable, directional, rotary, rhythmic, lastly chaotic form of its percolating time which associates, in it, the time of the heart and the head, of the clock and the barometer, of the periodic and the aperiodic – that crystal aperiodicity Schrodinger had divined in the science of the living is thus conducted back here, into the very experience of our proprioceptivity –, sine and turbulence... and, doubtless, other times we don't know of yet. Well-informed, doctors adopt the caduceus as their emblem: serpents and staff. Hence the expectancies of the female body.

From Life Toward the Soul

Do I have a more remarkable recollection than my university championships in the high jump? A handsome Malian giant with tall and slender musculature, Tiam Papa Gallo always beat me, with a smile, hands down, and I, without jealousy, saw myself as an insipid and solemn worm next to this archangel who, before my very eyes, broke the two meter mark, for the first time in France. Rolling three or four steps on his marabou legs, he took flight; he crawled. Why didn't I have the wit to call you Blessed Lightning? Dear and old friend Tiam, if, after your tribulations, life becomes agreeable enough for you to read me, you should know that, during those afternoons of grace, you taught me the ecstatic and fluent transparency of the human body. But, come to think of it, from the line-out in rugby to volleyball's spikes, from basketball defense to the goalie's aerial saves, from the scrum-half's diving passes to flights above the trampoline... cite a sport where one doesn't jump. Were they invented to succeed in levitating?

Transformed into obese pigs by the drug – soft in a hard way – consumption, we have been forgetting, for the past half-century, the extent to which our body knows how to escape gravity by obeying it. Ingestion to excess suppresses the spirit. Nearing the fall into the grave, I remember with elation that the body is woven of subtle breaths. Granted, it tumbles and slides down the walls on which it risks its life, should it lose its grip, but after having learned the ways of balance in and through a hundred vertiginous rotations, it can and knows how to take flight. Of low density, pierced with sluices, conduits, networks in which fine fluxes circulate, floating, dancing, speeding on wheels, aerial, the flesh, of density close to water, floats and even takes off with no trouble; everywhere porous, full, in the chest, of oxygen's happiness, light ɔf bone, articulated with new circles in its upper body: shoulders, arms, neck, occiput, wingspan... even more than in its lower body, inspiration dilates it with air, sight penetrates it with light, heat fills its skin to make it limber, elastic muscles lift it, nerves tense it with attention, the voice exalts it, and the erection invites it to levitate... there it is, conversely, converted toward the vertical.

If we write *flux*, we ape the scientists, while *breath* exposes us to the risk of being considered long-winded or worse, today, for spiritualist; it's, nevertheless, a question of the same circulations. Breweries of liquids and gas, molecules, electrical or chemical signals, many an exchange between our open and gossamer membranes and the fluent world follow complex cycles, cycles whose fluidity delicately takes over from the coarseness of the solid wheels articulated to the lower limbs, whose simplicity I just now described, a simplicity that, all of a sudden, compared to the vortices engendered by these mixtures and tenuous communications, seems crude. Perched or raised upon wheels, we find ourselves, now, more skillfully, riding at altitude on a thousand cycles, whose multiplicity cooperates, combined, toward temporary and continually taken up again equilibria but that intoxicate, I imagine, even more than swings or waltzes, with their currents of oxygen, alcohols, endorphins, calls or information... we know more people drugged by Coke and newspapers than stupefied by gymnastics, dance and the high jump. Just as we found bearing's uprightness through the vertigo that pulled us toward the ground, so too amid these numerous and subtle vortices belonging to the internal environment or the innumerable exchanges with the surroundings, we obtain, the most often, something like the suspendedness of a bird whose almost motionless wings rest upon invisible turbulences, like a constancy soaring over incalculable multiplicities.

From the riddled body, porous, shot through with just as many epicycles whose combinations bring about more and more delicate subtleties, the vertical soul emerges, is born, springs up, or from the lightened flesh, the flying spirit. The animate or the spiritual (translated by our languages from the breath of the winds) emanates – light vapor – from the body's most immediate proprioceptive experience: from the solid circulations and gaits of walking first, then from the balanced exchanges of the energies received or produced by the countless cycles of the metabolism. Our light casts incorporeal signals into the mists, so that we may inhabit, for life, the tenuous tissue of dreams. And, past my time amidst the signs, I shall vanish from above like the fog.

Leaving

Do you remember the day you quit your mother's womb, and what shrill call pulled you from your warm bath, sleepy and solitary? This exit twice begins anew. When a new life with respect to the life of childhood is invented, and strange places, a strange time and social circle settle around your decisive will, between the ages of fifteen and twenty-five; take heart, friend, and I shall lend you my arm to cross the ford. My hand searches for yours but doesn't find it, for, far away from me, you see before you a mountain torrent, whose mouth I gaze on at sea level. It's my turn, now, for the other stage.

This yellow broom, these black pines in the clear sky, this dense silence within the wind's bass, the beauty of the lines of the hills, at the horizon, the suspended meditation of space and the melancholy of the rain, the heart's secret and vertical exaltation amidst the body's pains, the immensity of the world into which I am diving, enraptured – life, little by little, has put me here like the embryo in the liquid-filled cavern, after several heartrending separations. At the same time you're giving birth to your life, it's delivering itself of me. It's going to come out of you; I'm going to come out of it. Strange outlet, death expels us from the exterior: how does one leave the outside? How does one become separated from things themselves separated?

Just as the baby at term obeys the calls of the maternal skeleton and pulse, beatings of a clock preceding the native alert, I already hear the creaking of the world's exertion, with an eye to my expulsion. Since I have never, indeed, seen such soft tints on the rocks and among the flora, nor heard such secret harmony in the breeze and across the sheets of fertilisine, nor was ever caressed so by the spring winds and the eddies of water, such a serene body to body equilibrium between the universe and the organism must mark the swan song, the absolute perfection of the musical chord, at the end of the sonata. When the deviation is reduced to repose, that deviation whose disquietude, a little bitter, launches into enterprises and impels into the islands of strange seas, when the slope that courage climbs or that soaring joy descends, grows level, the landscape rejoins the soul in even equanimity, while the soul, objective and corporal, reaches all things. Motionless, knowledge comes to completion, in that it makes the external and the inward depths indiscernible. My absence will be hidden in the open exterior, scattered, like ashes, amid the totality. Forge your density from this world where mine is being lost.

Thus we live without miracle the lessons of He who, after having willed the Incarnation, ascended, as the Scripture says, into rarefied skies.

THE VERTIGOES OF KNOWLEDGE

The form of the foot, its active circular unfolding, the pains and pleasures of those who devote themselves to Ilinx games and the rhythmic arts, or entrust themselves to machines with pedals, to be sure, but above all to the pure wonders of the sailboard, the hang-glider, the parasail... so many apprenticeships to the space of grace our language calls mind. Fearful, we believe we owe our equilibrium to stiffness, to the right angle and the square, more at ease seated, lying down, static or flabby than standing and in motion and, suddenly, discover our error, when the mere act of walking shows us to be riding on arcs of circles and when other transports put us into ecstasy after the initiatory pain. The vortices give stumbling toddlers and inexpert adults this vertigo – bad, at first, delightful, later and a long while – that we rediscover, sometimes, when we learn, anew, how to ride a bike, the waltzer in her dance or the boat in the repeated volute of the waves. Pedestrian or foot soldier, we were walking, slow and heavy, and, suddenly, we find ourselves on bicycles, in music or at sea, discovering that formerly, while we were dragging our clumsiness along on foot, we were doing, less well, what, precisely, we are doing now. Walking appears, then, to be a particular instance of the motion of the pedal, the waltz, the keel of the vessel or aerial turbulence.

As they sang in times past, Mommy, will the boat have legs, or, miracle, will we walk on the water?

This corporal vertigo – witness of the continuous passage from a stiff equilibrium to a second state, paradoxal and refined, then another and another still, all stable after a different manner through unexpected motions – is experienced with each entry into a world that disorients us and with the encounter of a new logic, unforeseen, that surprises our habits apparently from behind, but which, nevertheless, perpetuates, by discovering them, the body's complex *habituses*. The intoxication, real, of knowledge and intelligence, the mystical elation of inventive discovery follow the joys of the bicycle and the swing, of the aircraft and the forecastle, wind in the hair... of the pitching and rolling of reunited lovers.

An Origin of Geometry

So open your body up to the vertigoes of intelligence. In Euclid's *Definitions*, for instance – that is, its first lines, even before the axioms and postulates, and throughout their refined sequence – the Greek language constructs more and more complex and subtle equilibria, from the simplest, lying on the ground, at the lowest of low points, and by continued inclinations, increasingly high and vertiginous, toward the plane and the four-legged table, then toward the circle and its diameter, all the way to he stance – the most paradoxical – on the point of a rhombus or diamond, the vertical axis of the top, whirling and vertically turning. One would almost think that these first lines recount and summarize in ten formal words, for the quickest – because the most abstract – understanding, the long history of *Homo erectus'* thousand and one acts of straightening up, taken up again by the child learning to walk, then to run, by the mountaineer who begins climbing, by the courage that faces, by Jesus transfigured, by Thales standing in the shadow of the pyramid, discovering his theorem... and by the athlete running the hundred meters: life continually invents – like at its beginnings – new equilibriums, unstable and rare.

The *Origines de la géometrie* (pp. 251-259), which carefully describes this construction, following the idea of a mechanics, already rational, therefore anterior to geometry itself, had, by distraction, forgotten, among the most immediate emergences, but no doubt the most concealed by the ignorance we stand in of the body, which is nonetheless sometimes cited by scholarly language when it speaks of legs in order to define the isosceles and the scalene or knees to express their angles, had, as I was saying, forgotten this experience of walking and stance, with the same elevation, the same learning, the same passage from lying flat toward a vertiginous cycle on the extreme point of a diamond. And, incidentally, physics begins, for the Epicureans and Lucretius, with a tremendous vertical fall, interrupted by the vortices which, as I have shown long ago, engender things. The way opens from the body to life, from life toward the mind, lastly to the truth of the sciences.

The Mathematical Body and the Toise: Space and Time

The cubit, inch, pace and foot... these old units referred to the body, as though it measured all things; aware of the exquisite way in which the body sets about evaluating the signals it receives, contemporary physiology confirms this ancient intuition. These units have the advantage of convenience. The metric system, on the contrary, abandons the body-subject, adopting, for example, the measure of the Earth or the wavelength of a certain atom: science replaces the subjective with the objective. Among the old units, the *toise*, equivalent to six feet or around two meters, pronounces in French the Latin *tensa*, the feminine past participle of *tendere* – in French *tendre* [to stretch] – from which the terms *extending* or *extension* are derived, as though these latter encompassed everything that can stretch out. So the subjective measure, the toise, is expressed by the same word as the objective measured, extension. Or, on the contrary, since, as we now know, muscular and articular sensors evaluate tensions, don't these words acknowledge that these measures emanate from the body-subject? How to decide?

Furthermore, the Latin *tendere* refers, in turn, to the Greek τεινω, *tendre* or *tenir* [to hold], once a serious rival of τεμνω as the source of time: scholars went around saying that they were wavering between an etymology that stretched out continuous duration and one that cut it up into discontinuous elements in order to measure it. So formerly the same origin simultaneously held space and time. The first displays tensions and continuities which distinguish it poorly from the second. Contenance signifies capacity or volume and *maintenant* [now] holds the present instant in the hollow of its palm more than it marks it: these two fraternal words indeed originate in the same ancestor ten. While tension can be described as a rigidity or an elasticity, tenacity or attention, what preconceived ideas then persuaded certain philosophers to oppose extensive extension to intensity?

Since a tensor can be defined in as many dimensions as one pleases, it can be conceived for a space-time, the very one in which the body runs and stretches out. A tensor of the first order, does not the vector itself, scan at will the one or the other, since it plots a movement, the one and the other? Einstein discovered space-time thanks, in part, to the calculus of tensors, thus this latter finds again, in a rigorous language governed by mathematics, the intuition of a spatio-temporal toise. Language spreads its branches and roots as though it has long known that our body also functions like a tensor; not the brain, as had been believed, but the body. Since each of its postures presupposes and masters equilibrium, movements, stretchings and torsions, as well as the measures of their variations, these vectorial functions must be generalized to a tensorial integration.

THE EFFORT OF STRETCHING

Even bending, I can't reach the cup; but, without getting up from my chair, I stretch my arm again and reach the handle with ease; I even had to turn my wrist a little more so I could grab it in its upside down position. To get the socket wrench over the head of the hard to reach bolt, I have to twist my shoulder. Likewise: how do we get to the out of reach hold in climbing? What pianist has forgotten that by practicing the span of his hand passed the octave so that his little finger can hit the E beyond? Past the free-fall, by how much do we grow, upon the sudden shock, when the parachute opens?

Movement, it is said, characterizes the animal; man's supple plasticity is added to it, but this elasticity only enables metamorphoses, work and even emotional expression because of that element of fine capacity, which we share with other animals, to add, certainly not cubits to our height, but a few centimeters to our limbs and muscles and a few minutes of angle to their joints, at the very maximum of their action: we can count on a surplus. Ductile, they twist, tighten and lengthen without breaking, beyond stretching. In extension and rotation, we enjoy a margin of tolerance, moreover. Better than the way the bowstring or the moorings of a ship stretch taut, we thus benefit from a supertension. Without this superductility, we could not catch, on the mountain face, those out of reach holds, nor could we vary on the ways of gripping them, straight on or undercling; without this margin, who could dance, what yogi could meditate? Manual dexterity, in work or art, makes use of it. Stretching taut remains a distinguishing feature of mankind, or its pretension. That legendary bandit the Greeks called Procrustes, "he who stretches out by lengthening," laid, as the mythology tells us, his victims out on a – different – bed, on which he forced them to go to the extremes of this power, by stretching what is too short and cutting what exceeds, thus becoming the reference for torment and exquisite torture. Between the loves and the tortures, our body experiences its limits.

In the same way, like *extension*, the term *effort* expresses this surplus. Beyond the strength or force that pulls, the effort of stretching makes use of this supplement of length and angle, variable but limited,

limited but variable: a little more still, a little more...
It doesn't just implement our strength, but will make
use of this excess. Thanks to it, we do what we can't
do, reach the inaccessible, pull out the badly placed,
extract and clear the impenetrable, skirt obliqueness.
The body teaches us this surplus, in which all
excessiveness, perverse or divine, develops like an
embryo. It knows how to go beyond and elsewhere.
That's a fine proof of our potential and power.

What can the body do? More? Who knows? Yes
and no, it depends on the interval, that of Procrustes
and that of the pianist, which practice, precisely,
widens; are you going to reach the E? No and yes. If
yes, life booms and joy wells up. But before preaching
ethics and this surpassing, remember that, even with
muscles and desire stretched taut to the point of pain,
you never succeeded in reaching impossible loves.
And what if the mind were born of this crevasse
which one does not know whether one will fill?

So admire your mathematical body: lying, vertical,
leaning, spinning round and round, the skeleton
plays a referential role for a coherent extension,
by axes, points, planes and symmetries; the semi-
circular canals of the inner ear project information
regarding equilibrium and movement onto three
perpendicular planes; situated in the muscles and
joints, sensors are less about measuring position than
speed, acceleration and jolts, that is, the first, second and

third derivatives of the magnitude in question; the set of these differential elements becomes integrated in proportion to the rise of the neuronal networks toward the brain... the body functions therefore as though it took into account Euclidean geometry, Cartesian and polar coordinates, infinitesimal analysis, vector spaces such as tensorial calculus.

When I was describing Thales upright and standing, attentive to the meridian sun, at the foot of the Great Pyramid, did I understand just how much he was obeying the most secret promptings of his body? As though he were being transpierced by the sun god Ra's radiographic light, had I observed enough the transparency of his skeleton, the vestibule of his hearing, the calmed tensions of his calf muscles? Did he feel, at noon, Euclidean extension come forth, in full armor, from his tensed thighs? And who would have dared to connect the account, by Leibniz, of his infinitesimal intuitions to the circumstances of his long wait, at the mouth of the Thames, where contrary winds detained him for several days, studious of his algorithm amid the volubility of the rolling? Thrown into a thousand shifting inclinations, predictable and unpredictable, his muscular sensors were evaluating two or three orders of differentials: *him, too*.... No, the *petites perceptions* don't apply the new calculus to the body, the new calculus arises from them.

Do you want to invent mathematics? Consult your body, the devil take Plato; the sublime philosopher claimed that the ignorant slave, as staged in the *Meno*, had forgotten that he knew geometry, while the theory of the Forms hid from its author and two thousand years of servile mimicry this glaring truth: all bodies know geometry and each is ignorant of it. Blind to the body's riches, we don't even see what those who do see them are doing: creators owe their discoveries to an exquisite proprioceptivity.

Commodalism and Modality

Poincaré gives a lay explanation of this fact: he claims that we invent a given type of geometry or mathematics, because, more convenient, it fits our relations with a world in which solid objects are in congruence with our body. Euclidean geometry comes out of the skeleton, projective geometry from sight and topology from the skin.... Certainly. Certainly, a given site ties around itself, like an interchange, the set of paths we could take to get there. In saying this, Poincaré only defines a certain group of geometry. But our goal isn't just to go toward places: we also imitate the things that reside in them; we play them; we try to catch them, when they run away; we eat them, delicious, caress them, delectable, attempt to avoid them, when they threaten, or, trembling with desire, to attract them... so many behaviors, so many tensions and movements, so many metamorphoses. The body doesn't change solely in order to move, it transforms for a thousand other possible actions; it fails, when some impossibility stands in the way; then, it reacts to this contingency and, should it lose, resigns itself to the necessary, enduring it, contemplating it or, better still, producing it.

Consequently, Poincaré's commodalism – a popular variant of the positivist questioning: how, *comment, quo modo* – conceals a philosophy of modes: possible, impossible, necessary, contingent. Not just stable, like Condillac's statue, our body is continually moving: sight, as I have said, is only understood by a visit on the move, and Molyneux's blind man recognized the cube or globe by shifting his fingers a long while over their surface. Not just moving or moved, our body is continually assuming a thousand unexpected forms: it transforms. Far from stability, it moves; far from movement alone, it changes; unpredictable, these metamorphoses, sometimes necessary, often possible, occasionally impossible, can only be defined as contingent: here again we find the four categories of modality. Just as the body infinitely generalizes Poincaré-style movements, so this latter term generalizes, in turn, his commodalism. On balance, the body cannot be reduced to either a fixity or a reality: less real than virtual, it aims at the potential, better, it lives in the modal. Far from a being-there, it moves; it doesn't merely travel the course from here to there, but forms, deforms, transforms, tightens and stretches, figures, disfigures, transfigures, polymorphous, proteiform... you'll only stop these variations by defining it as capable. It can. This capacity sums up, like an indefinite integral, the open set of postures and grimaces, bearings and positions. I would even gladly define the body as a pre-position: precondition for every position and preparing them all. We have just considered only *vers*. Consequently, should it remain true that the other branches of mathematics are linked, more or less, to a lesser or greater degree, to one position or another, to one movement or another, to one tension or another, I find myself nearing the project of a *mathesis universalis* that would correspond to this fluid capacity.... Yes, Plato was truly mistaken when he invented the intelligible heaven where the Forms reign; for, just as concrete as the body, abstract mathematics enters the modal order.

We believe the body to be real and concrete when it's frozen into the program of a single set of positions; so, we create the mind as the universal set of all programs; but the human body can be defined, precisely and simply, as capable of every possible metamorphosis; if it doesn't execute them to perfection, it knows how to imitate or simulate them. Thus the mind-body dualism, so praised formerly, so rooted in mathematical invention – since this always leads, for example, to possible sets – so detested today by correct thinking, is resolved by the human body's capacity to enter into modality. In the same way, there is indeed, in computers, a software-hardware distinction, which appears, from a distance, to reproduce the mind-body duality; but, to be quite precise, software is as material as hardware.... The entire interest of this distinction consists in the variation of software for a given piece of hardware. Thus the body can receive and make use of as much software, as many postures and torsions, positions and movements, as one could want.

More and better still, evolution itself appears to be, like the body, of the modal order: the impossible sorts among the possible and makes the contingent appear as necessary. The sciences enter the same framework, for they continually play between the possible, the impossible, the necessary and the contingent: life, modal like the body; sciences, modal like living bodies.

Envoi: The Buoyancy that Makes Fly

For the simple story of Archimedes' most famous discovery to have come down to us, unchanged, across two millennia of history, generally false, it must conceal rich treasures.

Here's the naked engineer, in his bath. His body, floating, undulates, alone, in the volume, like a toy boat in a small tub where his limbs, naked, endeavor, a little, to float on the surface, given over to the slight pitching and rolling. Who sees there the work of some understanding, whose useless existence no one had yet suspected in those subtle times? No, there's a completely naked body, transparent fluid, and, before long, a theorem of equilibrium by means of the waters.

I've found it, he yells... and there he is, come out, still naked, into the street, shouting and running; naked, in the agora, to the great astonishment of the stiff, dressed, political people, motionless and standing, who see without seeing, streaming with water and light, a body and only a body, which now dazzles me with its truth value; naked, like the day he came out of his mother's womb and leaping like a child; naked, without any other apparatus, in the bath, on the ground and through the air, this body sinks but surfaces, rolls but floats, prey to the vertigo of drowning, but saved from the waters by that vertical force, it stands and steps out of its bath, walks, runs, leaving the tracks of its wet feet on the sand; finally, leaping with joy, takes flight, by following, in the wind, the *trouvaille*'s seraphic verb: *eureka*!

Eureka! I've found the vertical force that lifts the body rolling in the water, he shouts. But what power pushes it in addition out of the water, vertically still? *Eureka*! I say, in turn, for here is Archimedes' theorem generalized: every body honestly plunged into authentic life and into direct and courageous learning receives from them a force equivalent to this body directed upward, vertical, toward discovery. Amid the spins and the vertigo, we never find anything but while naked. Lifted by joy.

Who experiments? The body. Who invents? It does. And who floats, runs and flies, with archangelic intoxication when the blessed intuition bathes it and makes it levitate? The body, yes, the body again. Naked. Steeped in logic and memory, both mechanical – so leave them to the machines – intelligence remains stupid and heavy without it, winged.

Ascension: it has just cast off.

Univocal Publishing
123 North 3rd Street, #202
Minneapolis, MN 55401
www.univocalpublishing.com

ISBN 9781937561062

Jason Wagner, Drew S. Burk
(Editors)
This work was composed in Minion.
All materials were printed and bound
in November 2011 at Univocal's atelier
in Minneapolis, USA.

The paper is Mohawk Via Linen, Pure White.
The letterpress cover was printed
on Crane's Lettra Fluorescent.
Both are archival quality and acid-free.